The Paideia of God

The Paideia of God

and Other Essays
on Education

DOUGLAS WILSON

Canon Press

MOSCOW, IDAHO

Douglas Wilson, *The Paideia of God and Other Essays on Education*

© 1999 by Douglas Wilson
Published by Canon Press, P.O. Box 8741, Moscow, ID 83843
800-488-2034 / www.canonpress.org

Unless otherwise indicated, all Scripture quotations are from the New King James Version of the Bible.

An earlier form of "The Paideia of God" appeared in *Tabletalk*. Many thanks to them for permission to repeat and strengthen the point. "Why Evangelical Colleges Aren't" first appeared in *Chronicles*. Many thanks to them as well.

ISBN: 1-885767-59-5

Contents

Chapter One:

The Paideia of God

The work of rebuilding Christian education in our culture is a massive task, but nonetheless it has been undertaken by thousands of parents and teachers in countless homes and classrooms across the country. Those who are involved in this work of restoration are usually familiar with Paul's great words of exhortation on fatherhood (Eph. 6:4), which is good, but we have now come to the place where we must go beyond a mere familiarity. Paul's requirement here is actually one of the most far reaching commands of the New Testament, and we need to understand why this is so.

Paul says in that place that fathers are to take care to bring up their children in "the nurture and admonition of the Lord." While this is taken vaguely by some as an exhortation to "be a Christian dad," others rightly see the words as more pointed than this and assert that Paul is specifically requiring Christian education for the children of Christians. I believe this is correct, but we must also come to see that much *more* is involved in this requirement than simply establishing the scope and sequence of a formal Christian education.

First things first. In our day, we need to make sure we can see the big E on the eye chart right at the start. We may then proceed, in the latter part of this essay, to squint at that troublesome line near the bottom. So this is why we must always begin with understanding the necessity of a Christian formal education for our children.[1] But this is really just the beginning. The fact that many thousands of Christian parents still have their children in the government schools shows how far we are from even *beginning* what Paul requires of us. And although many have abandoned the practice of allowing secularists to instruct their children, we must never forget that this is just a good start.

In Ephesians 6:4, Paul is in fact requiring Christian fathers to provide their children with a "paideia of the Lord." Now if we were to describe our process of education to a first century Ephesian and then ask him what Greek word would be used to describe this process, the initial answer would be simple and straightforward— *paideia.* This is not an obscure word or concept; the idea of *paideia* was central to the ancient classical mind, and Paul's instruction here consequently had profound ramifications. I say the *initial* answer of the Ephesian citizen would be simple because what we call education is more strictly a mere subset of *paideia.* Formal education is essential to the process of *paideia*, of course, but the boundaries of *paideia* are much wider than the boundaries of what we understand as education. So our helpful Ephesian would tell us that *paideia* is certainly the word we are looking for, but he would then think for a moment and go on to tell us that it is not quite that simple. In short, their *paideia* was broader, bigger, deeper, and far more developed than our notions of what constitutes "education."

So while this means that our verse could appropriately be rendered in a way that required Christian fathers to bring up their children in the "education of the Lord," we are not done. Far more is involved in this than taking the kids to church or having an occasional time of devotions in the home, as important as such things are. And more to the point, far more is involved than simply providing the kids with a Christian curriculum, 8 to 3.

Werner Jaeger, in his monumental study of *paideia*, shows that the word *paideia* represented, to the ancient Greeks, an enormous ideological task.[2] They were concerned with nothing less than the shaping of the ideal man, who would be able to take his place in the ideal culture. Further, the point of *paideia* was to bring that culture about. To find a word of comparable importance to them, we would have to hunt around for a word like "philosophy." To find a word of comparable importance in our culture, we would have to point to something like "democracy." The word *paideia* was as central to the thinking of the Greeks as the idea of the proletariat is to a Marxist, or cash to a televangelist. It was not a take-it-or-leave-it word like whatever the original Greek word for shoelaces was.

So the word *paideia* goes far beyond the scope and sequence of what we call *formal* education. In the ancient world, the *paideia* was all-encompassing and involved nothing less than the enculturation of the future citizen. He was encultured when he was instructed in the classroom, but the process was also occurring when he walked along the streets of his city to and from school. It included walking by the temple for the gods of his people. That too was part of the process.

If we bring this down into the present in order to illustrate what it would mean to us, *paideia* would include the books on the bestseller lists, the major newspapers, the most popular sitcoms and networks, the songs on the top forty lists, the motion pictures seen by everyone, the architectural layout of most suburban homes, and, out at the periphery, the fact that all our garden hoses are green. When we look at the current governmental support of our *paideia*, we see that the classroom activities of goverment schools would certainly have to be included and placed at the center of the process. In those classrooms, the message of "tax-supported anything but Christianity" comes through loud and clear.

But the center of the *paideia* in the classrooms does not complete the relation of *paideia* to the schools. We also see, all over the country, other aspects of our modern *paideia* that are connected to formal education. For example, children by the million stand along the side of the road and then climb on to their yellow school busses—or as the educrats might want to call them, "motorized attendance modules of distinctive coloration." This common experience is also part of our secular *paideia*, and part of our process of enculturation. Because of it, I, who grew up in Maryland, have something in common with someone who grew up in Oregon. To make the process complete, we were also taught the same kind of foolishness when we got to school. So this process is occurring when secular dogmas are taught, and it is occurring in our practice of having first graders write on wide-lined paper with the bark still in it. So then, *paideia* is not just bounded education, it is enculturation—every aspect of enculturation.

This leads to the next issue, the ramifications of which are enormous. I want to argue here that it is not possible to fully provide "the paideia of the Lord" outside the context of a Christian civilization. If this is the case, then Paul's command to the Ephesians, when they did not live in a Christian culture, just as we do not, means that he saw, at some point in the future, the necessity of establishing a Christian culture. And this also means he saw the provision of Christian education as being closely related to the formation of this culture. The establishment of Christian schooling necessarily entails the establishment of a Christian culture. Culture is not possible apart from a *paideia*, and *paideia* (in the fullest sense) is not possible apart from an established culture. We have ourselves a chicken and egg problem. The fact that Paul commands fathers to begin a Christian process of enculturation means he saw, with the eye of faith, the end result, which would have to be a Christian culture. Outside the context of a particular kind of culture, the word *paideia,* as it was used in such contexts in the ancient world, makes no sense.

The theoretical and practical problems associated with this are, of course, great. In our day, the idea of Christian culture is suspect, even among Christians, and many within the Church are consequently advocating what they call "principled pluralism." In their minds, it is good that the broader culture is not Christian. And even among those who see the blessing of Christian culture, there are wide differences of opinion on what exactly that might look like. And so we need to be patient and study the issues as carefully as we can. Unfortunately, we do not have a lot of time.

We have seen in the last generation, with the explosion of Christian academies and the parallel explosion of homeschooling, something which the parents involved thought would be culturally "neutral." They thought they were doing nothing more than saying, "Not with my kid, you don't." They thought they were doing little more than simply exercising a personal choice. But these parents were actually setting in motion a series of events that make it absolutely necessary for the Church to address the question of Christian culture. And they did this by establishing (with many variations between homeschools, tutorial services, and Christian schools) at least the faint outlines of a recognizable Christian *paideia.* And this means the pressure is on. What next?

Because it is impossible to build a successful system of education that does not require a surrounding culture, the rise of Christian education is creating (whether we want it to or not) a demand for Christian culture. If we do not confront this looming reality and prepare ourselves for it, the time will come when we find ourselves in the midst of a Christian culture, but it will be a bad patch job—a Christian culture because Christians are in positions of influence and power but not Christian in the biblical sense. This has happened before, more than once, where the saints found themselves in possession of a culture for which they were not really prepared. The results have included some unhappy consequences. Every thinking Christian ought to be grateful for the settlement of Constantine and for the influence of the Puritans in England. But we would have to be blind not to notice that a premature arrival of Christian culture can easily set us up for a fall.

The wheels are coming off our postmodern culture, like it was Pharaoh's chariot, and we should not be surprised when we finally see the deliverance of the Lord. To alter the picture somewhat, neither should we be surprised when we find ourselves in possession of vineyards we did not plant and wells we did not dig. This is God's way. But we are supposed to prepare ourselves for that time so that when it arrives we are not astonished—and unprepared.

The *paideia* of a true Christian education is that necessary preparation. This *paideia* prepares for and ushers in a true Christian culture, and once that culture is established, the *paideia* of God is the ordained means for maintaining that culture as it prepares young Christian children to assume their station within Christendom.

But we must know and, more importantly, understand the potency of what we are doing. I am very encouraged by what Christian parents have been doing with the education of their children but very distressed that they have not seen the cultural potency of what they do.

While the *paideia* is not limited to formal education, we certainly see that formal education is right at the heart of *paideia*. It does not constitute the whole of the thing, but it does occupy an influential and controlling position. This is why the government school system has been so important to the secular project in America. As long as the children of Christian households attended the government schools, their distinctive cultural quirks could be tolerated as just that—eccentricities of a subgroup within a broad and diverse culture. Whenever students share the same formal education, their cultural differences become mere *subcultural* differences. And this is why, until recently, evangelical Christians have operated with a ghetto mentality, maintaining a thriving subculture that was simultaneously ubiquitous and impotent.

We have all sorts of distinctive things to ourselves—our own network of radio stations, our own network of bookstores, our own bumper stickers, and so forth. And yet, the Christianity exhibited has just been another minor flavor in the multicultural casserole. This is because the children of most of those who listen to Christian radio have their kids in the government schools. The children of most of those who frequent our Christian bookstores make sure their kids are taught differently at school. In our postmodern culture, the polytheism inherent in the diverse culture can certainly accommodate one more clown in the circus ring. What they cannot accomodate is a true alternative, which is starting to take shape.

Christians have not presented a true cultural alternative until recently, when they began to provide their own children with an education consistent with what they believe. The reaction of the secularists to all of this shows that the children of this generation are often shrewder than the children of light. They know—far better than we do—what is actually at stake. They fear, rightly, the *paideia* of God.

Chapter Two:

Teaching Disa*d*ilities: Why Johnny Doesn't Learn Much Anymore

Understanding Our Situation

The entire subject of learning disabilities is a delicate one. Of course no one wants unnecessarily to distress parents who are already having a difficult time with the education of their children, but at the same time, the current and received wisdom on this topic is becoming more and more questionable. We are certainly confronted with a multitude of children who are not "getting it," but we must also acknowledge that this multitude of struggling students has appeared at just the time when our education system is in crisis, with some portions of that system already in ruins. Is this simply a coincidence, or is there a connection? We have always had schools; why have we suddenly been confronted *now* with a small army of the "learning disabled"? The answer is not necessarily to be found within the students.

If it is our schools which are "teaching disabled," the symptoms of this lack would still be visible primarily in the students and not necessarily in the schools or teachers. When a doctor is incompetent, it is still the *patient* who dies. If we think about this situation carefully, we should acknowledge that the location of the symptoms is not necessarily the location of the problem. The purposes of this small essay are to consider our tidal wave of learning disabilities and to call us to reflect on the possibility that the real problem is one of *teaching disabilities*. Are our children failing, or are we failing our children? In light of the monumental failures of our government educational system, the time has come to consider the latter as a real possibility. Indeed, when the evidence is carefully weighed, such a conclusion appears inescapable.

The Current Scene

The words have certainly not been slow to enter our everyday vocabulary. Dyslexia, learning disabilities, hyperactivity, Attention-Deficit Disorder (ADD), Attention-Deficit-Hyperactivity Disorder (ADHD), and not a few more have all become commonplace in discussions between parents of school-age children. Some parents have their kids on Ritalin, others have their children in special tutoring programs, others have their children in special counseling programs, and many of the rest of the parents find themselves nodding sympathetically. And those who are *not* sympathetic are frequently afraid to say anything about it for fear of giving offense.

Classrooms with a large percentage of the students on Ritalin—a purported treatment for ADHD—are not uncommon. Out of America's 38 million children between the ages of 5 and 14, about 1.3 million children take the drug regularly. Rare is the conversation between parents on the subject of education that does not end with a discussion of the various forms of learning disabilities. What the entire subject cries out for is a large infusion of biblical thinking and common sense. Do we really believe that this epidemic of learning disabilities is the result of our *superior* ability to diagnose problems? Do we think we are better at educating our children than previous generations—those generations which were able to impart near universal literacy? If we really think so, then perhaps *we* have the learning disability.

Consider the fact that our "better classroom discipline through chemistry" approach has become necessary at just the point in history when parents and teachers *en masse* have abandoned the biblical view of the nature and necessity of discipline. Consider the fact that the "medical problems" associated with reading problems have soared at just the point in our history when educators have abandoned the time-honored and time-*tested* method of teaching literacy through phonics. Consider the fact that we have adopted the medical model for just about everything that afflicts us at just the time when we as a culture have rejected the importance of personal responsibility and accountability for anything.

Within the last few years, the use of Ritalin has soared. Programs for special needs students have multiplied. And as this generation of children has grown up in an environment of institutionalized excuses, it is supremely ill-equipped for maturity. Not surprisingly, many adults are now insisting on bringing their baggage—in the form of notes from their doctor—along with them. We now have *Adult* Attention Deficit Syndrome. And why not? Modern man is in full flight away from maturity, responsibility, and hard work. At the rate we are going, I would not be surprised to hear that specialists have identified Manual Labor Dyslexia. "This poor fellow really should have an indoor job. He can't identify the working end of the hammer."

The Language of Medicine

In this general flight from maturity, our culture has taken a dislike to any words which carry the aroma of praise or blame with them. This dislike is applied both to the categories of character and gifts. Where Johnny used to be lazy or inattentive (each being worthy of reprimand), we now find that he has ADD, which is more like having the measles than having a character deficiency. Where he used

to be disobedient or wild, he now is a hyperactive or
strong-willed child. We may perhaps be forgiven for thinking the problem is actually weak-willed parents and not
strong-willed children. With regard to gifts, where Johnny
used to be slow or backward, he is now "differently-abled."
Of course, this is not written as a defense of the cruelty
that was sometimes inflicted in the older days, when children were sometimes mocked for their native inabilities
and taunted for a failure to be intelligent enough. But at
least this older cruelty had the virtue of honesty—in stark
contrast to the cruelty of lying to a child for twelve years,
all for the sake of his self-esteem, knowing that at some
point any child with less ability who has not been taught
well will be blindsided by an unforgiving reality, whether
or not his ignorance was excused by the appropriate authorities at the time.

   No one thinks of blaming a child for coming down
with a cold or for catching the flu. Since the medical model,
or syndrome system, offers refuge from responsibility, we
have not been slow to seek out that refuge. This desire
to have a medical or scientific name for our child's condition springs ultimately from a deep-seated egalitarianism.
Whenever we use the language of praise and blame, in this
lumpy and uneven world that praise and blame is invariably distributed in uneven amounts. And for an egalitarian,
such unevenness is always "unjust" or "unfair." Because
it is unfair and because modern educators are driven by
a leveling desire, believing that each student has a "right"
to the same results as any other student, something must
be done about this unevenness. Whenever parity of result is denied for various reasons (usually related to how
God made the world), something has to be done about
it. Driven by envy, the language of "rights" and medical
excuses is commonly found in the mouths of our educators. But in the world God made, equal efforts do not result
in equal results. This is why our modern school system
is structured around the desire to sandpaper out all the

inequalities—this explains the lower academic standards which virtually all can meet, and it explains all the "notes from the doctor" which excuse the remaining deficiencies. Thus everyone comes out more or less at the same place, or so we believe, and as Gilbert and Sullivan put it, "You are right, and I am right, and everything is quite correct."

It is true that in the real world, hard work is blessed by God and laziness is chastised. But the blessings are hardly ever in direct mathematical proportion to the effort expended. Some students sweat bullets over their homework every night in order to eke out a B minus. Another glances at the study sheet fifteen minutes before the test and aces it. This difference in student ability is one of the reasons why our government school debacle is not a whole lot worse than it already is. Even though most schools do not teach phonics anymore, some students are bright enough to teach themselves phonics—but of course these are the kids who could teach themselves to read by staring at their cereal boxes every morning. Whether we are talking about academic ability or any other kind of ability—musical, athletic, social, etc.—life is simply not fair. Any educational process which refuses to take these inequities into account is doomed to ignominious failure. Further, any school which refuses to *honor* these inequities is going to fall.

Because egalitarianism is false, we must not expect that a reinstitution of discipline and standards in our schools will result in every student replicating the labors of Hercules in the halls of the academe. Every teacher since the beginning of the world has known that some students are bright and some are slow. Some are naturally industrious and some are not. When strict standards are applied in any school, some students will soar and others will struggle their way through. *This is not a sign that something is wrong.* Neither is the possibility or even *necessity* of failure for some students an indication that the school is not doing its job. Those who want a risk-free world, a world in which failure is impossible, desire a different world than the one into which they were born. Those who want failure-free schools for some students want schools that in no way prepare any students for life.

The fact that one student has to work twice as hard as another student in order to get half the distance is not an abnormality. I was once speaking with a mother who was wanting to excuse her son's behavior because of certain circumstances which she believed were rigged against him. I did not agree with her, but her assumption led to an interesting question. She believed that her son was living in a world where he would have to work doubly hard to get the same distance as his peers. I pointed out that he was currently working *half* as hard. What did she think was going to happen to her son? In the world God made, excuses are a thin armor.

Discipline

Discipline is not an end in itself; it is the fence that, in a fallen world, protects that which has value. A school without discipline is a school with AIDS—the school has no means of protecting itself from misbehavior or academic laziness, which means it has no way of protecting its mission and its reason for existence. The school has no immune system to fight off those infections which will destroy the school in substance, if not in name also. A lack of discipline will spread from the students to the staff, and it will not be long before the school is filled with teachers and students, each providing cover for one another's laziness.

Moreover, a refusal to discipline teaches students to treat the education being offered with contempt. The students will certainly despise any education that the educators themselves hold in contempt. And if parents and teachers refuse to discipline, they are holding in contempt the education they offer. A man who refuses to defend his wife does not love her, does not value her. An educator who does not defend the process of education is in the same position. And his contempt for the education offered is contagious—it will spread to the students. Without discipline, education in a fallen world is impossible.

The Bible teaches us something very important about the nature of discipline: "Now no chastening seems to be joyful for the present, but painful"(Heb. 12:11). Whenever any son or daughter of Adam encounters academic discipline, they are not discovering something that is necessarily "fun." The ground, since Adam, has never yielded its fruit without labor. School work is, well . . . work. But because, as Neil Postman has observed, we have adopted the entertainment model of education ("as seen on TV!"), whenever we run into this uncomfortable thing called work in our studies, we think that something has gone wrong. If it is boring, it must be bad. And whenever we think that something has gone wrong we *ipso pronto* hustle our children off to a specialist, who discovers that they have LOWS (Looking Out the Window Syndrome). The entertainment model of education wants the students to enjoy *themselves*; the older classical model wants students to be disciplined so they come to enjoy their *work*.

If we insist that every moment of education be "fun," whenever the inevitable large amount of necessary work sets in, we must conclude that something is seriously amiss, particularly if the students have learned that it is profitable to yelp. And whenever something is seriously amiss, we need some sort of scientific name so that we can all feel better. What would happen to Tom Sawyer in today's government school system? There is little question that he would be diagnosed with ADHD:

The harder Tom tried to fasten his mind on his book, the more his ideas wandered. So at last, with a sigh and a yawn, he gave it up. It seemed to him that the noon recess would never come. The air was utterly dead. There was not a breath stirring. It was the sleepiest of sleepy days. The drowsing murmur of the five and twenty studying scholars soothed the soul like the spell that is the murmur of bees.

And Huck! Huck Finn would be on the brink of institutionalization or perhaps locked in the recesses of some alternative high school, having been hit on the head with a chemical rock.

Biblical discipline has both positive and negative aspects. In neither case is it punitive. Punishment is interested simply in justice; discipline is interested in the twin aspects of preparation and correction. When students are made to work hard, this is preparation for life. When a student is corrected for fooling around and wasting time, this is correction that returns the student to his preparation for life. In both cases, the purpose and function of the discipline is to *prepare* and *correct*. But with punishment, the purpose is justice. When the civil magistrate executes a murderer in obedience to the law of God, the point is not to make the murderer better. But when a son is spanked by his father, the point is the peaceful fruit of an upright life.

Positive discipline does not presume that the student has done anything wrong or has been disobedient. Setting the student on a course of studies, making him complete his work on time, establishing goals that will be difficult for him to meet are all forms of discipline. This course of study is what makes the student a *disciple*, one subject to a pattern of discipline. The vast majority of education is discipline in this positive sense. A student may spend years in a school without ever being sent down to the principal's office. But he must not spend years in a school without submitting to the course of study set for him. This shows us that while correction may be absent for a self-motivated and well-behaved student, discipline is never absent.

Negative discipline is a response to wrongdoing. Its purpose is to protect the positive discipline. Negative discipline corrects the various forms of behavior that threaten the course of positive discipline. The positive discipline instills character and knowledge over time. Whether the problem is laziness or simply inexperience and immaturity, the problem is corrected over time by the work that is done. And negative discipline steps in as necessary to protect this process against any behavior which threatens it.

Whenever the various excuses supplied by "learning disabilities" are used, the result is the destruction of both positive and negative discipline. And the result of *that* is the destruction of education, which is what we in fact see all around us. Without discipline there are no disciples, and without disciples or students, there can be no education. This abandonment of discipline is not hard to understand—work has always been hard, and sinners have always sought ways to get out of it. In addition, whenever someone shirks their work, the initial response is to invent excuses. The excuses may be believed for a while, but time is a great revealer. *The abandonment of discipline is the abandonment of disciples.*

For example, when a student discovers that an assignment is "hard" and verbalizes his complaint, relief can come in various forms. If he finds a sympathetic ear in his parents or teachers, he will not be slow in verbalizing his difficulties the next time. For someone who is supposed to be learning-disabled, he actually learns very quickly. "Work is unpleasant, and this gets me out of it."

Once this pattern is established, negative discipline disappears quickly as well. How could it not? If a student is prevented from completing the assigned work by forces outside his control, it would be an outrage to chastise him for falling short. And with this "atmosphere of excusing" surrounding him, excuses can be offered for more and more bizarre behavior. Beginning with excuses for a wandering mind, we end with excuses for rape, assault, and murder. The evidence for this is as close as the nearest newspaper.

Phonics

With discipline lost in general, we should not be surprised when particular aspects of academic discipline are lost. The teaching of reading is not rocket science. For all its quirks, English remains a phonetic language, which means that the sound of a written word may be decoded, left to right—provided the sounds that correspond to the various letters have been mastered by the student. And there are not all that many sounds to master.

When phonics are not taught, some bright students will nevertheless figure out the general phonetic pattern by themselves. But many of the students will begin a lifelong struggle with their "learning disability." The tragedy is that many students who were fully capable of learning to read and write very well will be saddled with the consequences of someone else's blunder. Just as a poor coach blames his team, so a failed education establishment has taken to blaming the students. It is worth remembering that these students were coerced into coming to these schools through compulsory attendance laws, made to sit in a desk for twelve years, and then graduated without being able to read their own diploma. Or, since the student is told *he* is the one with dyslexia, he is unable to read his own biqloma.

In the "look-say" method of teaching reading, which has evolved into what is now called the "whole language" approach, the children are not taught to master the individual sounds of the individual letters. They are shown a picture, say, of a chair, along with the letters c-h-a-i-r.

Some students, as mentioned above, figure out the phonetic connections. They remember that *chair* and *church* have a similar squiggle at the beginning of the word and that the two words have a similar sound at the beginning. But for those students who are not systematically taught the connections between the letters and sounds, it is not surprising that many of them do not master the connections. Neither is it surprising that others, attempting to memorize a complex squiggle of lines, confuse some of the letters that have a similar appearance. They mix up the b's and d's, or the p's and q's. When they do, they may find themselves hauled off to a program for dyslexics before they know what has hit them.

For those who already know how to read, the fact that a young novice might struggle with the concept is difficult to grasp. When the novices *do* struggle, this is taken as evidence that something unusual is going on—some learning disability must be at work. But imagine what it would be like to try to learn a bunch of words, the letters of which did not have any phonetic relationship to the sound of the words. Suppose the sound *chair* were represented to you by a random collection of Japanese letters unfamiliar to you. How would you go about memorizing this? Do you think that you might get any of the letters backward while you are memorizing lists of words that have no apparent pattern or key to them? The fact that English words *have* a phonetic pattern is of no help at all to a student *who is not taught that it has a pattern or what that pattern is.*

Evidence of this particular teaching disability can be identified if a student looks at a word of any length, say, *barbarian,* and reads out loud something like *banana.* This reveals that the student was not taught that every letter has phonetic significance, and that when confronted with words like this, he believes he should simply take his best guess. What is being done to students under the influence of this "progressive" form of education is criminal.

Wanting It Both Ways

The idea that one's child has a learning disability dies hard. I have seen many classical Christian schools start up in response to the failure of the government schools. It is not surprising that many Christian parents are attracted to such schools; they have high standards for their children and they are seeking out schools with which they may share such high standards.

Another class of parent is discontented with the government schools, but for some reason such parents have nevertheless continued to believe the government school's diagnosis of their child's learning disabilities. Their discontent is attitudinal but not defined and focused. In other words, the parents will often become disenchanted with the fruit of excuse-making long before they are prepared to reject the excuse-making itself. Thus they come to a private school because they do not like how their learning disabled child was treated, but they continue to insist that their child *is* in fact learning disabled. They then insist that the private school respect the diagnosis but do a better job than the previous school did in addressing it.

But any school which structures its program around learning disabilities is going to spend a great deal of time chasing its tail. If learning disabilities are the problem, then the solution must be new and innovative methods of teaching—to try to solve the new problems presented by the student. And this is just what we find in those schools that follow this pattern. Schools are constantly fixing on this or that, as they follow "the latest developments in education" that will enable us to deal with these learning problems. The modern education world is really a world of fad and fashion. But if learning disabilities are really teaching disabilities, then the solution is for schools to return to classical excellence in teaching. Outstanding teaching has existed in the world for millennia; we have no need to wait for the invention of anything new. The answers are in old and musty books, in the experiences of older teachers who have managed to ignore all the latest foolishness, and in a humble admission that while modernity does not know how to educate, our elders did. Modern education assumes the problem is in the student and spends a lot of time and money endlessly tinkering with him. Classical education assumes the problem is with our lust for innovation in teaching methods and strives to refine a tested adherence to the old. Fortunately, this is a debate that can be settled by pointing at a scoreboard. Which students know how to read? Which students can think? The answers to such questions are not as mysterious and hard to understand as some want to make out.

But making this distinction plain is not possible if classical schools structure their program in any way to accommodate those who have believed the lie of "learning disabilities." When the school forms, it must take special care to establish and *defend* (remembering the importance of discipline) a responsible policy on learning disabilities.

Learning disabilities should be divided into two categories, the first of which may be called severe and medical. A severe learning disability is one that (beyond dispute) has a medical basis and would require a special classroom, teachers, equipment, etc. in order to enroll the student. "Disabilities" in this category would be things like blindness, deafness, mental retardation, and quadriplegia. Most private schools, when they are first starting, are not able to establish such programs for obvious financial reasons. And if they cannot accommodate such students, then the policy should plainly state that they cannot. Some parents with a special interest may be motivated to begin such a program. If they are and the project is financially feasible, then of course it should be undertaken. At the same time, the school should be extremely wary of such programs, because it is very easy to get tangled up in federal money. And when one gets tangled up in federal money, he is also tangled in federal regulations and controls. He who takes the king's coin becomes the king's man.

The other learning disabilities are those that this essay has been primarily addressing—dyslexia and all the other alphabet disorders. When a child has been "diagnosed" with some such disability and the school has been informed of this by the parents, this probably means that the parents expect the school to take special account of that disability in time spent on the student, grading standards applied to the student, assignments given to the student, etc. The school must make it plain *before the student is enrolled* that every student admitted is held to the same standards.

In doing this, the school does not have to argue with the parents over whether the dyslexia, say, is real or not. If the parents believe the diagnosis, they are free to obtain whatever tutorial or medical help they desire before or after school. But if they want their child enrolled in this school—a school seeking a return to high standards and few excuses—then they must understand that the standards of the school will not bend to accommodate them.

This requires a few words about parental authority over education. One of the foundation stones in the resurgent classical school movement is that God has given authority over the education of children to the parents of those children, not to the civil authority and not to the Christian church. Neither is this authority given to a Christian school directly—the school functions as a servant to the parents, with the authority to educate delegated to them temporarily *in loco parentis*. In Deuteronomy 6:4–9, God requires the parents to teach their children to love Him with all their intellect. In Ephesians 6:4, the apostle Paul requires fathers to bring up their children in the *education* and admonition of the Lord. Christian education is not an option, and parents are responsible for it.

This being the case, then how can I argue here that schools should ignore the concerns of parents who believe their child is learning disabled? The answer is found in the nature of corporate servanthood. When a school establishes itself to serve parents by teaching certain subjects to the kids, this does not mean that any given family has complete authority over the school. What happens is that the school clearly notifies the families of a given community what service they intend to offer to them. Those parents who want that service may avail themselves of it, and those who do not will not. But parental authority does not mean that one family has the right to demand *another* service entirely. If a man started up a Burger King to help parents feed their kids, parental authority does not mean the parents have the right to come in and order a Big Mac. In the same way, if someone wants to start a Christian educational service that believes and accepts all the various diagnoses of learning disabilities, he is completely free to do so. But I do not think business will be all that good; the more we believe our learned doctors of education, the worse our problems get. A free market in education will never produce the follies we see in the government school system. We see private schools and homeschools springing up all over, we see programs like Hooked on Phonics, and we see Sylvan Learning Centers. All these are an intelligent response to the disasters caused by the government's teaching disability. But we will never see a chain of Dyslexia Underwriting & Mentoring Businesses (DUMB). *That's* a job for tax money.

What Do I Do?

It would be nice if parents who learned these things could put them into practice regardless of how old the children are. But the point made earlier about failure in education applies equally to parental oversight of education. Not to put too fine a point on it—it is possible to screw up.

The earliest years of a child's education are the most critical. It is here that teaching disabilities can cripple a child for life. I have spoken before with parents whose children were enrolled in a good Christian school at around the third grade, and they are still struggling years later because of how their children were taught in the first several years of their education.

Suppose some parents have a twelve-year-old son who is functionally illiterate and has been diagnosed as a dyslexic. Whenever he has to read anything, he labors through, taking five times as much time as any of his classmates—and furthermore, he doesn't really get what he reads. His parents need to arrange tutorial help for him—help which will teach him what he should have learned *in the first grade*. If he did not learn it there, he will never encounter it naturally at any other place in the curriculum. No one will take a semester out in tenth grade to go over "how to read."

In some cases, the failure is complete and the parents can do nothing about it. The child who was not educated is now grown and away from home. In other cases, parents learn what they need to know when the children are still toddlers, and they can provide what is needed. And for many others, they must work through the "good news" and "bad news." The good news is that the situation is remedial. The bad news is that fixing it right will cost time, money, and a good deal of commitment. But the greatest cost is that of learning to walk away from *all* excuses. There is no shame in having, loving, and teaching a slow child—if that is the way God made the child. But there is a great deal of shame if *we* are the ones who, through our folly, have retarded the child. As we look around at the wreckage of our schools today, there is a great deal to be ashamed of.

Chapter Three:

A Brief Statement Against Vouchers

As government education continues to deteriorate across the land, plans to save it have not been wanting. To this date, one of the more popular approaches to "reform" looks to be vouchers. Under most voucher plans, parents of school-aged children would receive a voucher from the government which could be "cashed in" at the school of their choice. This voucher could be spent at public or private schools, and even at religious private schools.

For the purposes of this essay, vouchers refer to government vouchers, although there are some successful privately-funded voucher plans in operation also. Against such private plans I have nothing negative to say. The money involved in the plans is not my money, and those who do own it appear to be doing charitable and kind things with it.

But government vouchers are in a different category entirely. Christian educators, who stand to benefit greatly from any wide-ranging voucher plan, need to understand both the theological and practical reasons why they must stay completely out of any public voucher programs.

This discussion does not directly address other alternatives, such as tuition tax credits, which are not as bad as vouchers but are still bad enough to oppose. When the government grants a tax credit based on tuition paid out, it is a small step for them to begin inquiring as to whether the institution receiving the tuition is worthy, or accredited, or whatever. My three children went through twelfth grade without anyone from any government agency knowing where they were attending school. That is the kind of situation every parent who loves educational freedom should long for. It was a great blessing indeed.

In my judgment, the possibility of that blessing spreading to many more families is threatened by the various voucher proposals more than any other thing. In some places my language may seem strong, or even intemperate. It is not my purpose to be insulting, but I see a monstrous threat here, and no other response is really possible.

First, the theological case against vouchers should be made, and here it is: "You shall not steal" (Ex. 20:15). We have grown comfortable with the statism we live under, and one shameful result of this is that we have been trained to accept "the taxpayers's money" as though it were a monolithic entity. But the "taxpayers' money" is actually Smith's money and Murphy's money. It was taken from them with the threat of violence. Why should it be given to me?

The Bible teaches that the civil magistrate may require a certain level of taxation (Rom.13:6–7) and that Christians are required to pay those taxes cheerfully. But the Bible also teaches that civil authorities are capable of breaking God's law, including His prohibition of stealing. Even if Ahab had had his wits about him and gotten hold of Naboth's vineyard through land reform or a rezoning maneuver, we would still know what to call it—stealing. Samuel informed us what the threshold of economic tyranny is when he told the Israelites that if they called a king like the other nations, he would eventually begin taxing them at ten percent (1 Sam. 8:15–17). We, in the grip of our ignorance, think we would be as free as the birds if we got back to *that* level of tyranny. For many of us, the tax burden is approaching fifty percent.

No wonder it's hard to think straight. But it seems curious to me that at just this time, many Christians are calling for another program that will need to be funded. Trying to get it up to sixty percent?

Lawful taxation occurs when the civil government levies a tax to pay for those things that God requires it to do. The civil magistrate is God's deacon, as Paul teaches in Romans 13, and is assigned to punish the wrongdoer and reward the righteous. When they are about their assigned business, that costs money, and Christians should be eager to pay their taxes. But when they abandon their assigned duties, and begin to reward the evildoer and punish the righteous, that taxation becomes theft. This essay is not calling for tax revolt—a refusal to pay taxes because I am being stolen from. Rather, the point is that we should stop clamoring for yet another program that would require the government to steal still more. The reason we are stolen from is that we are thievish at heart; God judges us according to how we treat others. The measure we use is measured to us. I pay exorbitant taxes because somewhere, someone else is yelling for a program. If *we* start yelling for a program, it hardly looks like repentance.

I should not be willing to receive a voucher for the education of my children because it is not right for the magistrate to threaten another man with prison time to make him willing to pay for the education of *my* children. To this the reply might be made that the recipient of the voucher pays taxes too. Right, but if each taxpayer only received out what he paid in, the system would collapse. The system works because everyone comes to it hoping to get more than what they paid in; that is, they come with theft in their hearts.

When the government is involved in the redistribution of wealth, the government is stealing. When the citizenry calls for the government to redistribute some wealth, the citizenry is aiding and abetting that theft. We see this principle clearly when it comes to food stamps, welfare checks, and so forth. We just do not see it when we might get something.

Second, vouchers will simply change the nature of our educational slavery; they will not usher in educational liberty. Instead of the educational socialism we have now, we will have educational fascism. In the former we have public ownership, in the latter we have private ownership with public control. And when Christian schools are controlled by the secularists, the results will of course be predictable. In his case against vouchers, Jack Phelps provides some good summaries of how the one who takes the king's coin becomes the king's man.[1] The man receiving the money rarely knows this. *The one giving it always does.*

The future of education in our nation is slipping through the secularists' fingers, and they know it. They can't educate, and those who can educate do not answer to them. Their once proud system is in ruins. What to do? They would rather own all education outright, but if they can wield control over private institutions, that is sufficient for their purposes. Those Christians involved in building schools who do not see what a potent threat to the *status quo* their schools are need to stop and think the issues through. Vouchers threaten the financial independence of Christian schools at just the time when that independence is most necessary.

Third, vouchers expose the essential hypocrisy of many of our attitudes on public policy. Educational vouchers are nothing but food stamps for conservatives. It is remarkable how often we do not see the *principle* involved. We simply react to some "wasteful" program, defining wasteful as "someone else getting the money." Until we learn to fight statism by refusing to accept *benefits*, our hypocrisy will be evident. Anyone can complain about having to *pay*; where is the distinctively Christian worldview in that?

A biblical worldview is not seen in a reluctance to pay

high taxes. Rather, a biblical worldview is seen when we understand *why* there are high taxes.

Fourth, to argue in favor of vouchers in our context requires that Christians argue for the one thing we must not argue for at this point in our history—the myth of neutrality. Education is inherently religious. Vouchers that can be spent at a Christian institution are in effect a subsidization of the Christian faith. The same would be true of a Muslim school, and so on.

The way around this—when the vouchers are issued by a pluralistic government—is to argue that the subsidy is directed toward the neutral part of the educational process and not toward the chapel or Bible classes. But there is no neutrality, and there cannot be any neutrality. There are only two options for the advocate of vouchers: he must either say that the government should support Christianity whole and entire (and Islam, and Buddhism, and atheism) with tax money, or he must say that there are significant portions of the curriculum at this voucher-receiving institution that are not distinctively Christian and that the secular government may therefore support.

So we either have to grant that we may be taxed so that a Buddhist parent may be funded to instruct his kids that Buddhism is true, or we must say that Buddhist education and Christian education are the same for *most* of the day. Support for vouchers among Christians reveals that we have not yet learned the central lessons of all Christian education, which are the myth of neutrality and the necessary antithesis throughout all time between belief and unbelief, at every level, in every place. In short, those Christians who advocate vouchers for Christian schools should not be trusted to run Christian schools, because they do not yet understand the central lesson to be learned there. They should not run Christian schools because they should be attending one.

And lastly, the acceptance of vouchers will perpetuate ignorance on the subject of economics. Given the state of the modern world, this is a bad area in which to further ignorance. Schools on the dole will have absolutely no incentive to instruct their students about God's laws concerning wealth and poverty, charity and industry, economic love and hate. They will have no incentive to show their students the important distinction between seen effects and unseen effects. This incentive will not be there because a bright student in the back of the room might ask an embarrassing question. "Why do I get to come here on a voucher then?"

In summary, as the reader may have surmised, I hold that vouchers are a bad idea, top to bottom, front to back.

Chapter Four:

The Biblical Meaning
of School Clothes

Our casual age wants to insist that how a student dresses
will surely have no effect on the operations of that
student's brain. Surely a student can learn and study and
memorize, without his wearing of sweat pants or jeans or
shorts interfering with the operation. At least this is the
way it seems, seeming quite obvious, to many.

But there are good reasons for challenging the assumption, and we need to challenge it soon. The standards
of our broader culture are not static and can be expected
to deteriorate further; we must think through the issues
carefully. If we do not, a common pattern followed by
Christian schools will continue—anything the world does,
we can do five years later and worse. But before proceeding
further, it would probably be good to begin with a defi-
nition; in this essay, *school clothes* are defined as being dress
that is designated as appropriate to a student's vocational
calling.

So is school dress an academic issue? The government
schools of a generation ago had stricter standards of dress
than many private schools of today. And if a school today tries to tighten up the standards of dress (e.g., "Boys,
tuck in your shirts."), the uproar can be considerable, and
not all of it from the students. Many times parents will
get into the picture, writing off those conservatives and
traditionalists who want the kids to "look nice" at school

as sartorial gnat-stranglers. "Why don't they just concentrate on teaching? What do torn jeans have to do with math?" And for many such parents, the issue is complicated because a school with higher standards of dress for their children can appear to be undermining their legitimate parental authority. "Why is a *school* telling my child how to dress?"

In order to answer the question, we have to consider several issues. The first has to do with the scriptural teaching on how decisions are to be made in voluntary associations like a school. The second is the direct teaching of the Bible on the subject of dress. This must be done in the context of some of the broader cultural issues we see around us. In other words, an item of clothing might mean one thing in one culture and have quite a separate meaning in another time and place.

With regard to the first issue, parental authority is not undermined when a school adopts certain general standards of dress—any more than when a school adopts a standard curriculum. The parents wield their authority as they make the decision to enroll their children and as they oversee the process of education the school has promised to provide. If a school promises one thing to parents but then secretly refuses to provide it, then the authority of the parents is being attacked. But if parents enroll their children in a school with a dress code, then the entire transaction is voluntary. Such voluntary restrictions—of many kinds—are taken on by every parent who enrolls his child in a school. The family agrees to have their child begin studying at a certain hour, from a certain text, in a certain subject, taught by a certain teacher. The only thing a dress code adds is the agreement of the parents to have the child dressed a certain way. If the parents agree with the school that such dress is conducive to a studious and disciplined atmosphere, there is no problem.

But before parents agree to this, they might want to consider what the Bible teaches on this subject. Now, the good life is characterized by the true, the good, and the beautiful. Believing Christians have done fairly well in turning back the modern onslaught against the first two. Some want to maintain that "truth" is a meaningless mental construct, but we serve the Lord who is Himself the Truth. When Pilate asked the famous question, "What is truth?" the answer was standing right in front of him. In the same way, the relativizing of ethics has been effectively resisted by believing Christians. If something is wrong, it is wrong all the time. If something is a sin, then it is a sin on Tuesday as well as Friday. The ultimate standard of what constitutes sin is found in Scripture, most notably in the ten commandments. As the apostle John stated it bluntly, sin is lawlessness (1 Jn. 3:4).

But on questions of beauty, order, and propriety, Christians have not done so well. In fact, the relativism that permeates our culture is manifested whenever Christians discuss aesthetic issues in any area—whether the subject is music, clothes, painting, or dance. If a man were to say, for example, that alternative rock music stinks, the reply that many Christians would give to him is very revealing. Their comeback is almost always a variation on "Who's to say . . ?" This is nothing other than an appeal to the authority of relativism. The claim that there is an area of our lives where the Word of God has no relevance, and hence no authority, is a claim that human standards must govern and rule in that area. But if human standards govern, and human standards shift and change, then this means that anything done in this realm is simply arbitrary and relative. If someone were actually to argue for the superiority (or adequacy) of alternative music by appealing to set standards of beauty, his reply would be a dignified one. Even if he is wrong, he is arguing like a Christian and a gentleman. But relativism is no reply at all, and on aesthetic issues, too many Christians have drifted into such relativism.

Consider the example of Abigail. When the Scripture

states that she was a beautiful and intelligent woman (1 Sam. 25:3), this means that, according to the Bible, by good and necessary consequence, there is such a thing as beauty and intelligence in women. This may seem like a commonsense observation, but relativism in aesthetics is constantly trying to undermine the obvious. When the Bible tells us we are to "sing to Him a new song; play *skillfully* with a shout of joy" (Ps. 33:3), this means there is such a thing as musical skill. The Lord has not seen fit to leave us with a sound recording of such skillful performances, but we know that skillful performances are *there*. In principle, we know it is possible to distinguish good music from poor music.

The Bible also tells us that nice clothes exist: "Then Rebekah took *the choice clothes* of her elder son Esau, which were with her in the house, and put them on Jacob her younger son" (Gen. 27:15). Rebekah was able to choose from a selection of clothes, and from that selection, she picked out what Jacob was to wear. What she picked out were the good clothes. Not to belabor the point, but this means that the expression "good clothes" is a meaningful one.

When God rebukes the city of Tyre through the prophet Ezekiel, He mentions one of the items they trafficked in: "These were your merchants in *choice* items—in *purple clothes*, in *embroidered garments*, in chests of multicolored apparel, in sturdy woven cords, which were in your marketplace" (Ezek. 27:24). Achan was tempted by silver and gold and *clothing*—"When I saw among the spoils *a beautiful Babylonian garment*, two hundred shekels of silver, and a wedge of gold weighing fifty shekels, I coveted them and took them. And there they are, hidden in the earth in the midst of my tent, with the silver under it" (Josh. 7:21).

Naomi instructed Ruth to keep this in mind when she presented herself to Boaz: "Therefore wash yourself and anoint yourself, put on *your best garment* and go down to the threshing floor; but do not make yourself known to the man until he has finished eating and drinking" (Ruth 3:3). The point being made here is a very simple one. The Bible reflects what we all know to be true—as long as we are not in a debate over school clothing—in our everyday experience. Some clothes are nicer than others. According to the occasion, some are better or more appropriate than others. Consequently, for a Christian, a straightforward relativism on the clothing issue is impossible.

Now an objection may come back at this point, which is that the Bible doesn't tell us what these choice clothes actually looked like. And if one of our eleventh grade girls showed up in Ruth's "best garment," she would undoubtedly be sent home for her outlandish behavior. So doesn't this mean that to look to the Bible for verses that talk about clothing is missing something important?

It is granted that cultures vary and that good clothes in one culture will not necessarily be considered good clothes in another. We are not arguing that we should find out what the apostles wore and then make our kids wear that to school. *We are after the principle, not the method.* For example, the Bible tells us to "honor all people" (1 Pet. 2:17). This is a constant duty in all cultures. But the method used to honor others will vary from culture to culture. Put another way, the Bible does not tell us whether the British or the American military salute is "more proper" than the other. But it does require the *fact* of the salute. Expressions of honor are common to all human societies, and the Bible requires that we honor others and maintain such expressions of honor. To allow cultural expressions of honor to fall into disuse and to forget them is to lose the vocabulary of obedience. Then, when we find ourselves needing to obey, we have lost the means to do so. Consequently, we must distinguish between the position that says (correctly) that expressions of honor may vary and the position that says there is no such thing as an expression of honor.

Now when this principle is acknowledged, which is that in any given situation, one way of dressing is better and more appropriate than another, and a course of action is taken in order to meet the requirements of the principle, the expression of the principle—whatever it is—is Christian. Two different schools on opposite sides of the country could adopt different methods of holding to the same principle—one school requiring polo shirts and the other requiring button-down shirts, for example. But as our relativistic culture drifts into expressions of clothing avowedly relativistic and therefore increasingly bizarre, and Christians tag along behind, wondering "Who's to say?," something is *seriously* wrong.

So we must look to the Bible for guidance on what sort of universal human realities are reflected and expressed by clothing. In looking for this, we are not trying to trap each person in one suit of clothes that is ideal for all occasions. Clothes vary, even on the same person, for the occasion. Every culture in the history of the world has recognized the categories of "work clothes" and clothes for more formal situations. A man should not rent a tuxedo in order to build a brick wall. His clothing is not suitable for the occasion. The Bible reflects this universal principle. John the Baptist lived in the wilderness, a rough prophet. His calling required suitable dress, and he wore camel's hair and a leather belt. This was in sharp contrast to another vocation—"But what did you go out to see? A man clothed in *soft garments*? Indeed, those who wear *soft clothing* are in kings' houses (Matt. 11:8).

The familiar biblical expression "gird up your loins" reflects the fact that clothing gets in the way of some activities. Besides the lesson of true humility, Jesus illustrated this at the Last Supper. He "rose from supper and *laid aside His garments*, took a towel and girded Himself. . . . So when He had washed their feet, *taken His garments*, and sat down again, He said to them, 'Do you know what

I have done to you?'" (John 13:4, 12). In a similar way, Peter showed that an outer garment was a nuisance while fishing. "Therefore that disciple whom Jesus loved said to Peter, 'It is the Lord!' Now when Simon Peter heard that it was the Lord, he put on his outer garment (for he had removed it), and plunged into the sea" (John 21:7).

We can multiply biblical illustrations of this general principle. How men dress is meaningful, not arbitrary. For example, in countless places the Scripture refers to men reflecting their sorrow and grief through their clothing: "Then Jacob tore his clothes, put sackcloth on his waist, and mourned for his son many days" (Gen. 37:34; cf. 2 Kings 6:30). In the same way, release from mourning is also shown: "So David arose from the ground, washed and anointed himself, and *changed his clothes*; and he went into the house of the LORD and worshiped" (2 Sam. 12:20).

We may show joy through our clothing—"Let your *garments* always be white, and let your head lack no oil" (Eccl. 9:8). Jesus told a parable that used the importance of social propriety as a lesson concerning the kingdom of God. "But when the king came in to see the guests, he saw a man there who did not have on *a wedding garment*. So he said to him, 'Friend, how did you come in here without *a wedding garment*?' And he was speechless" (Matt. 22:11–12). In the midst of a fierce rebuke, the prophet Isaiah recognizes the existence of *"festal apparel*, and the mantles; the outer garments, the purses" (Is. 3:22).

In biblical times, clothing also reflected societal status: "She shall put off *the clothes of her captivity*, remain in your house, and mourn her father and her mother a full month; after that you may go in to her and be her husband, and she shall be your wife" (Deut. 21:13). In the same way, a widow was identified: "So she took off *her widow's garments*, covered herself with a veil and wrapped herself, and sat in an open place which was on the way to Timnah; for she saw that Shelah was grown, and she was not given to him as a wife. . . . So she arose and went away, and laid aside her veil and put on *the garments of her widowhood*" (Gen. 38:14, 19).

We also learn in the Bible that clothing reflects a man's spiritual condition. One example is found when Jacob tells his household that they must serve the Lord: "And Jacob said to his household and to all who were with him, "Put away the foreign gods that are among you, purify yourselves, *and change your garments*"" (Gen. 35:2). And in the gospels, in the incident with the demoniac in the tombs, the problem with his nudity does not appear to have been one of sexual modesty but rather a rebellion against any restrictions of civilized behavior. The demoniac could not be bound with chains, houses, or clothes. "And when He stepped out on the land, there met Him a certain man from the city who had demons for a long time. And he wore *no clothes*, nor did he live in a house but in the tombs" (Luke 8:27).

We find that in Scripture, salvation is frequently pictured for us in the image of wonderful clothing: "Awake, awake! Put on your strength, O Zion; put on *your beautiful garments*, O Jerusalem, the holy city! For the uncircumcised and the unclean shall no longer come to you" (Is. 52:1). Granted this is a metaphor, but what understanding of clothing is necessary to make the metaphor work? Can we imagine a comparable metaphor coming out of our breezy and casual approach to virtually everything? "Awake, awake! Put on your flip flops, O Zion; put on your gym shorts, O Jerusalem, the casual city!" In contrast, the loveliness of salvation is pictured by loveliness in clothing: "To console those who mourn in Zion, to give them beauty for ashes, the oil of joy for mourning, *the garment of praise* for the spirit of heaviness; that they may be called trees of righteousness, the planting of the LORD, that He may be glorified" (Is. 61:3).

We must fix it in our minds that there is no neutrality *anywhere*. Relativism is dangerous in all its guises. This is true of our clothes, and the Bible goes far beyond simple issues like modesty. Again, the point is not that we must find out what widows in the Bible wore and make our widows wear that, but rather that the Bible recognizes the universal human tendency to reflect important social realities through clothing. The debate over school clothing often causes us to overlook the fact that even in our modern egalitarian society we identify and categorize people by means of clothing. We do this with soldiers, sailors, postal workers, doctors, nurses, employees of fast food emporiums, judges, policemen, UPS deliverymen, football players, umpires, ice cream truck drivers, and countless others. So when we want to identify someone as a "student," we are doing nothing unusual, and we are doing something we see done in principle throughout the Bible.

Of course the Bible prohibits making superficial judgments on the basis of someone's dress. It says,

> For if there should come into your assembly a man with gold rings, *in fine apparel*, and there should also come in a poor man *in filthy clothes*, and you pay attention to the one wearing the fine clothes and say to him, "You sit here in a good place," and say to the poor man, "You stand there," or, "Sit here at my footstool," have you not shown partiality among yourselves, and become judges with evil thoughts? (James 2:2–3)

James teaches us that in the public worship of God, it is wicked to show this kind of favoritism or partiality. What is prohibited in worship is also good to avoid in our day-to-day lives—including our time at school. One of the blessings of a defined school clothing policy is that it helps parents and teachers fight the very common temptation among kids to disobey this passage. While this passage is sometimes cited in opposition to dress codes, teachers are unlikely to think that a student is godly simply because he is wearing a nice sweater. But students *frequently* dismiss other students with contempt because they cannot afford the right designer clothes or their sneakers bear the wrong logo. Far from encouraging superficial judgments, a school clothing policy is an important tool to help parents and teachers instruct the children in avoiding this sin.

The flip side of this is also obvious. The Bible says that preening oneself is out. Not only are we not to make superficial judgments of others on the basis of clothing, but we must also refuse the temptation to try to *attract* positive superficial judgments: "But all their works they do to be seen by men. They make their phylacteries broad and enlarge the borders of their garments" (Matt. 23:5). A very common problem in schools is the peacock problem of trying to be "cool." A set range of appropriate school clothing is a great help in teaching the students to avoid this particular temptation.

The Bible teaches that the dress of women is to be modest. This does not refer simply to sexual modesty (though it certainly includes it) but also requires the avoidance of ostentatious display. Paul says that women are to "adorn themselves in modest apparel, with propriety and moderation, not with braided hair or gold or pearls or costly clothing" (1 Tim. 2:9). Peter agrees: "Do not let your adornment be merely outward—arranging the hair, wearing gold, or putting on fine apparel—rather let it be the hidden person of the heart, with the incorruptible beauty of a gentle and quiet spirit, which is very precious in the sight of God" (1 Pet. 3:3–4). In a Christian school, dressing in a slovenly way is not the only possible problem. Overdressing is sometimes a difficulty as well; math class is not the social equivalent of the prom.

In all this, we must remember the centrality of peripherals. The point is not to favor the peripherals *instead* of the center. That would be the sin of majoring on minors, swallowing camels, and all the rest of it. Rather, the point is that on this question the Christian world has fallen into the fallacy of bifurcation. Either we emphasize the center and wave off the peripherals as unimportant, or we emphasize the peripherals and forget the center. But remember, the fruit—which Christ required for identifying the nature of a tree—is way out on the edges of the tree and at the farthest point away from the root. We must recover the notion that peripherals are central because the center is important. Of course we cannot cleanse the inside of the cup by washing the outside. But when someone is transformed on the inside, this will necessarily have ramifications on the outside.

The Bible requires public thoughtfulness and courtesy. Consider just some of the exhortations which call us to honor and respect others (1 Pet. 2:17; 3:7; 1 Tim. 5:17; 6:1; Eph. 6:2; Rom. 12:10; 13:7). As mentioned before, in giving these requirements, the Bible does not tell us exactly *how* to honor other people. But in many places, it does require us to do it. The Bible requires courtesy, manners, etiquette. Now manners can be described as love in trifles, love at the periphery. The almost complete absence of manners in our modern society—a peripheral thing, surely!—is a horror if we are thinking biblically.

But what does this have to do with dress? If our modern and casual approach to student dress is seriously questioned, the response invariably will include an appeal to personal ease and comfort. But whose ease? Whose comfort? Jeans and T-shirts are easier and more comfortable than button-down shirts, ties, and slacks. So the solution is obvious, right? Not exactly. In the first place, take another look at how casual dress is being defended. The standard is "ease and comfort," with the supposition being that a person's reasons for dressing in a particular way are, of course, necessarily personal; they are to be found within himself and *for* himself. Whenever a student is asked to justify how he dresses, the criteria produced are expected to be a matter of what he wants to do. But where did we get this idea that our clothing is to be justified by how it makes *us* feel? Why is self-centeredness simply assumed to be the only possible court in which we are to try such cases?

Suppose we accepted the criterion of comfort but pointed first (and far more biblically) to the comfort of *others*? Certainly a shirt and tie are less comfortable to wear than a baggy T-shirt, but the shirt and tie are certainly more comfortable for others to view. So the issue is not really comfort but *whose* comfort. In our casual, breezy "it-must-be-comfortable-for-*me*-to-wear" orientation, we have certainly inflicted far more eyesores on the passersby than previous generations ever did. Sometimes the assault is deliberate, with the wearer trying to be rude. In other cases, it is simply thoughtless. But in a school that has stricter dress standards, the comfort of the broader culture is served and greatly increased. Many teachers and students have been distracted by rudeness in the clothing of others. A judicious school clothing policy greatly minimizes the occasions of such rudeness.

On the one hand is an appeal to ease and pleasure; on the other is an appeal to duty. In the former, the student is told that his first responsibility of every day (in getting dressed) is to suit himself. In the latter situation, the student is taught to put the interests of a larger community ahead of his own. And because we frequently dress without giving a tremendous amount of thought to it on any given morning, these two differing orientations actually grow to reflect two completely different habits of mind.

Now when two different students with these two different habits of mind come to their studies, what will be the result? Before the question is answered, we have to digress for a moment in order to defend the legitimacy of generalizations. No doubt a clean and starched collar can prop up a blockhead, and unquestionably we have all met zealous and industrious students in sweatshirts and blue jeans. But generally, does discipline of dress carry over into other areas? Really, to ask the question is to answer it.

Still, objections crowd into our minds. Strict dress codes, or required school clothes, are caricatured as some form of tyrannical mind control. "We don't want to suppress our child's individuality." But why do we raise this objection over dress and not over penmanship? Why not say, as the government schools are saying, that we should just let the kids be personally creative in every area? The answer is that to discipline a mind is not to be equated with destroying a mind and, further, that to let a student teach and discipline himself "creatively" is tantamount to expelling him from school. A swifter and more honest means of accomplishing this would be to defenestrate the student at the first opportunity. A student is a disciple. An undisciplined student is, therefore, an oxymoron, a non-student.

We cannot return in education to a culture of the mind without that return having a cultural impact. We cannot isolate how our students dress from how our students think. Neither can we detach how they learn to dress in their calling as students from how they learn to think as students. People who insist upon dressing casually also want to think casually. And in a fallen world, thinking casually means being wrong more often than not.

Now what may we conclude in summary? First, the Christian school is an institution in which a large amount of work, work of a particular nature, is conducted. The school has authority to direct the manner in which that work is undertaken. The school authorities must remember to have the directives be consistent with the mission of the school. Write in cursive, use pen not pencil, don't bring CD players and headphones to school, and don't wear blue jeans. The directives should not include, for example, the requirement that students hop from class to class on one foot. These directives should be given with the *overall* tone of the school in mind. This answers those who point out that some students look better in blue jeans than others do in the required school clothes. Yes, some students look good in anything while others look bad in anything. But the issue is the *overall* tone of the workplace. Some students might actually study better during a free period if allowed to listen to music through headphones, but what would the general outcome of giving such permission be? The Bible shows in repeated places that dress varies with occupation or vocational calling. Attending school is vocational, and students should be dressed appropriately for academic work. This means we have to remember that kids in "nice clothes" can be as inappropriately dressed as the kids aspiring to grunge. A girl should not come to school in formal dress and heels any more than she should come to basketball practice that way. So the students in a Christian school have a vocational calling. The question before us is whether or not there is a suitable form of dress for this calling. The issue is not whether the Bible specifically requires khaki slacks and a polo for geometry students but whether the Bible recognizes the universal human tendency to create garments suitable for various situations and consequently assigned to those situations.

Secondly, the Bible tells us that clothing can be used to express mood—we communicate whether we are celebrating or mourning, whether we are glad or serious, by how we dress. Students in a school should be required to dress suitably on the same principle that prohibits them from glowering at the teachers. *How we dress is an important part of our demeanor.* And what should that demeanor be? What is suitable for school? The students should present themselves at school in a way that says they are disciplined, relaxed, academic, and serious.

Third, the Bible tells us that it is legitimate to mark someone's position in a particular culture or society by how they dress. Having students on the way home from school recognized as students is fully in keeping with a general human pattern, and is observed in Scripture and seen regularly in other situations. To illustrate, just imagine how unhappy the kids on the basketball team would be if we required them to *not* wear uniforms.

Fourth, the practice of requiring school clothes does not really encourage parents and teachers to make false judgments. Rather, it is far more likely to *discourage* students from the very common practice of making such false judgments. In reality, this issue is not about the adoption of school clothes or uniforms but about which kind of school clothing will be required and who will require it. Will the board and administration require khaki slacks and a polo shirt, or will the power base in the student body require Tommy Whosit's name to be emblazoned on every genuinely cool rump in the school?

Fifth, modesty and lack of ostentatious display are important features of Christian demeanor in dress. A school should be very much concerned with life together. In order to make this small society function, the students should be required to dress modestly and comparably. This means that clothing will no longer be the distraction that it can be when this issue is neglected.

And last, the Bible tells us that we are to put others first and not ourselves. To require politeness through dress is simply to ask parents to teach their children to dress for comfort—the comfort of others.

The work of a school is the discipline and education of the mind. Adopting a school clothing policy is not a distraction from this task but really a very important part of it. No longer is a principal confronted with having to send a girl home three days in a row for having a short skirt. No more does he find himself disciplining some students who were brought to his attention while missing the others who were wearing the same thing. He is relieved to find he does not have to make constant daily judgment calls. The thing has been simplified. The thing has been agreed upon. And the work of true education can resume undistracted.

Chapter Five:

Does Classical Mean Reformed?

The classical and Christian school movement is still very young, but it has grown enough to attract at least some attention from every corner of the evangelical world. One of the results of this growth is that more than a few people have observed that the movement appears to be predominately Reformed. This in turn provokes the natural questions, "Is this a requirement? Does a classical and Christian school *have* to be Reformed? And anyway, what *is* Reformed?" Because of different understandings of words and differing circumstances, the questions can be asked accordingly, with words like Calvinist, Presbyterian, and Protestant running around and adding to the general muddle.

To answer this question—"Does classical mean Reformed?"—before getting into all the explanations, the classical Christian school movement is, in fact, self-consciously in the stream of historic Protestant orthodoxy. Most of those involved are in fact Reformed, while some are Lutheran, and some are part of that vanishing breed, the vertebrate evangelical. Our identification with historic Protestant orthodoxy is signalled by, among other things, the fact that the statement of faith of the Association of Classical and Christian Schools (ACCS) contains the first two chapters of the Westminster Confession, the chapters on the doctrines of God and Scripture. So, excluded from the movement are Roman Catholicism on the one hand and broad, modern evangelicalism on the other.

So no, a school does not have to be Reformed in the narrow sense. But every school that attempts to join with us in rebuilding the ruins of Western culture should, at the very least, have a great, informed appreciation for one of the great foundation stones of that culture—and that is the reformational world and life view. At the very least, ACCS schools should expect to attract Reformed applicants for teaching positions and Reformed parents seeking to enroll their children. And it is my conviction that any school that is nervous about this or hostile to it cannot hope to maintain an education that presents any alternative to the foolishness of modernity.

Because we are Protestant educators, our role is to fight ignorance through teaching. Ignorance of history is always to be deplored, but it is particularly out of place among teachers and educators. We cannot afford to skirt these issues simply for the sake of keeping our education safe and superficial. If we do, then we are trying to keep a school open at the same time we are running away from one of the great questions, a question which has had a formative role in the shaping of nations, cultures, and centuries. The issues surrounding what we have come to call "Reformed theology" are perennial. They have arisen repeatedly in the history of the Christian church. And because it is one of those inescapable questions, it comes up in *every* culture. Pharisees and Saducees debated it, Muslims have debated it, and there is no getting away from it. Actually, there is one way to stay away from it, and that is to embrace the modern notion that, for the sake of the lowest common denominator, an educational institution should be sure to cook up some thin soup for her students. But our schools were founded because we were tired of thin soup. As classical educators, we should understand the importance of the great questions and the importance of history. We cannot afford to dilute either.

A Short History

As with many issues, the first three centuries of the Christian church do not give us great insight on this question. In the absence of any doctrinal controversy about it, the position of the early church is hard to pin down. There are many references to election and to free will. But everything came to a head with the eruption of the Pelagian controversy. The Church was forced to define terms when She had to respond to a clear heresy on the subject. This was supplied by a British monk named Pelagius (early fifth century). Pelagius reacted to a form of fatalism in the Church—a fatalism that sought to justify sin. He did so by teaching that there is no original sin—each man sins each time entirely by choice. He was challenged in this by Augustine (A.D. 354–430), who provided the church with the first great systematic presentation of the biblical doctrine of grace.

Augustine won the battle, and Pelagianism was condemned as heresy. But after Augustine died, the Church drifted into something called semi-pelagianism. Augustinianism said that unregenerate man is dead. Pelagianism said he is alive and well. Semi-pelagianism compromised by saying that man is sick and needs help but that salvation is a cooperative effort between God and man.

Throughout the Middle Ages, the issue was of course debated in the schools, but some form of semi-Pelagianism was the received wisdom. Nevertheless, there was dissent here and there. In the ninth century, a monk named Gottschalk was imprisoned for maintaining the doctrines of grace. A few centuries later, others arose within the Church, maintaining that man is dead in his sin and that nothing but the resurrecting grace of God can save him. Wyclif and Huss were among their number. These men who came before the Reformation have to be included among those who affirmed the total sovereignty of God over all things. This would include the Waldensians.

Then, the Reformation. *Post tenebras lux*—after dark-

ness, light. All the Reformers were united on this point.
For example, Luther said this in his debate with Erasmus
on the subject: "Moreover, I give you hearty praise and
commendation on this further account—that you alone,
in contrast with all others, have attacked the real thing,
that is, the essential issue. You have not wearied me with
those extraneous issues about the Papacy, purgatory, in-
dulgences and such like—trifles, rather than issues. . . .
You, and you alone, have seen the hinge on which all turns,
and aimed for the vital spot."[1] The vital spot for Luther
was the absolute sovereignty of God.

At the Council of Trent, in response to the claims of
the Reformers, the Roman Catholic church delivered a
series of anathemas to the Reformation. In their condemnation of the Reformers' doctrine, it can be seen clearly
that the Roman church adopted the semi-Pelagian position while condemning the Augustinianism of the Reformers. The Roman church also condemned the teaching of
Augustine in their condemnation of an Augustinian movement within their church called Jansenism. The most famous of all Jansenists was a man named Blaise Pascal.

The Protestants, however, stuck to their guns, and
the Reformation became the Augustinian wing of the
Church. But after some time, a Reformed pastor in the
Netherlands named Jacob Arminius (1560–1609) came to
reject the teaching of the Reformation on these points.
At the same time, he did not return to the Catholic church.
After his death, his followers presented a "remonstrance"
to the Dutch parliament. The result was the Synod of Dort
(1618–1619), which met for many months to respond to
the "Arminian" position. They did so by condemning it,
laying out five articles—"the five points of Calvinism."
The Arminian position was thus condemned.

Semi-Pelagianism did not successfully enter Protestantism until the rise of Wesleyan Arminianism
(Methodism) in England in the middle of the eighteenth
century. Recall that the Reformation had begun early in

the sixteenth century, and we can see that the historic position of Protestants was well-established for two and a half centuries before there were really any non-Augustinian Protestants. This pervasive orthodoxy included the American colonies, and it did not begin to erode in our nation until the early nineteenth century. In fact, with the rise of government schools and the fall of Augustinian orthodoxy, we can see that they passed each other on the road. If we think that we are going to successfully challenge the modern secularist educators without coming to grips with these issues, we are sadly deluded. We have to meet the issues involved head-on.

The Basic Issues

So we come now to a discussion of what the fundamental issues are. This is obviously nothing more than a mere summary, but it is nonetheless a place to start.[2] In this section I will address only two issues: God's sovereignty over creation and God's sovereignty in our salvation. The reason for including this doctrinal sketch is so that any discussion and debate concerning Reformed theology in our schools may proceed intelligently. I am presenting this material because it is my conviction that classical and Christian schools must either be Reformed or congenial to the Reformed way of thinking. Neither position can be sustained in the dark, and so we must outline what is at stake.

With regard to the first issue, most Christians do not have a problem acknowledging God's control over the physical creation. Not a sparrow falls to the ground apart from the Father, and He knows the number of atoms that make up the planet Jupiter. Consequently, we should spend our time looking at the two areas that give us the most problems. Does God control the free actions of human beings, and does God control sinful actions? The biblical answer to both questions is *yes*:

> But Micaiah said, "If you ever return in peace, the LORD has not spoken by me." And he said, "Take heed, all you people!" . . . Now a certain man drew a bow at random, and struck the king of Israel between the joints of his armor. So he said to the driver of his chariot, "Turn around and take me out of the battle, for I am wounded." (1 Kgs. 22:28, 34)

In this situation, God had said that something would occur. He then used the *random* act of an unknown archer to accomplish *His* purpose for Ahab. The point is clear; even those things that seem driven by chance to us are in the hand of God. Our lives are bounded by God. "Since his days are determined, the number of his months is with You; You have appointed his limits, so that he cannot pass" (Job 14:5). Until the time comes that God has established, every man is immortal. As far as God's determination is concerned, we cannot lengthen and we cannot shorten our lives.

Humanly speaking, can we? Of course—we can chain smoke or bungee jump with frayed cords. But whatever we do will not alter God's ultimate decree—whatever we do will be His instrument for accomplishing His decree. We have the same teaching in Psalm 139:16 in different words. Before we existed, our biography was already written.

God's sovereignty extends also to those things we do and say before we get to our dying hour: "The preparations of the heart belong to man, but the answer of the tongue is from the LORD" (Prov. 16:1). What is more indicative of a man's freedom than that which he wills to speak? When you ask me a question, I answer you the way I wish. Is God somewhere else? No. God is sovereign over our free choices, and we do not have to explain the mystery. We just have to confess that the Bible teaches both.

But what about sinful words or actions? Does God control those as well? The reason we have a problem with God's control of free actions is that we do not want to say that men are nothing more than puppets. The reason we have a problem with God's control of sin is that we think that this would make God sinful or the author of sin. But first, look at the teaching of Scripture. Joseph clearly understood the goodness and sovereignty of God: "But as for you, you meant evil against me; but God meant it for good, in order to bring it about as it is this day, to save many people alive" (Gen. 50:20; see Is. 45:7 and Amos 3:6). God controlled, for His own good purposes, the sinful envy of Joseph's brothers.

The denial of Peter was also settled before it happened—"Jesus said to him, 'Assuredly, I say to you that today, even this night, before the rooster crows twice, you will deny Me three times'" (Mark 14:30). The treachery of Judas was in the same category—"And truly the Son of Man goes as it has been determined, but woe to that man by whom He is betrayed!" (Luke 22:22).

Everything about the passion of our Lord was ordained, and that ordination included the sinful (and free) actions of those who set themselves against Christ—

> For truly against Your holy Servant Jesus, whom You anointed, both Herod and Pontius Pilate, with the Gentiles and the people of Israel, were gathered together to do whatever Your hand and Your purpose determined before to be done. (Acts 4:27–28)

They gathered together to commit a heinous crime, but they only did what God's hand and purpose had settled beforehand. We therefore see that God can control sinful actions without being defiled by those sinful actions.

Of course, objections crowd into our minds, but they are not textual objections—at root they are philosophical objections. But the Bible says what it does.

When we come to the condition of man—and the salvation offered by God in Christ—we see that the sovereignty of God does not withdraw into the background. The same assumptions that the Reformed faith makes about the greatness and liberty of God in discussion of providence are also seen in any discussion of redemption.

First we must consider the condition of man. The nature of the "problem" dictates whether or not there can be a solution, and if so, what that solution will be. Among evangelical Christians, the nature of the "problem" of salvation can be described in two basic ways. Either man is sick in his sin, needing to take the medicine, or he is dead in his sin, needing to be resurrected.

Because all men are free agents they are free to do as they please. But because they are sinners, what they *please* to do is sin. This is why they need to be saved:

> For from within, *out of the heart of men*, proceed evil thoughts, adulteries, fornications, murders, thefts, covetousness, wickedness, deceit, lewdness, an evil eye, blasphemy, pride, foolishness. All these evil things come from within and defile a man. (Mark 7:21–23)

As creatures, men are free to do as they please. As sinners, men are not free to do right because they are constrained by the sinfulness of their nature.

The Bible expressly describes this unregenerate condition as being one of death. This does not mean that unbelievers are dead in every respect, but with regard to spiritual things, they certainly are—

> And you He made alive, who were dead in trespasses and sins, in which you once walked according to the course of this world, according to the prince of the power of the air, the spirit who now works in the sons of disobedience, among whom also we all once conducted ourselves in the lusts of our flesh, fulfilling the desires of the flesh and of the mind, and were by nature children of wrath, just as the others. (Eph. 2:1–3)

A dead man is in no shape to prepare himself for resurrection. He is impotent. When Christ raised Lazarus from the dead, it was not a cooperative effort between the two. Christ raised him, and *then* Lazarus came forth.

Another picture that excludes autonomous "free will" with regard to salvation is the picture of slavery. Dead men do not walk out of the grave, and slaves do not walk away from their masters—"For when you were slaves of sin, you were free in regard to righteousness" (Rom. 6:20).

There are no autonomous seekers of God. We all know that people do not become Christians unless they seek the Lord. The debate between Christians is therefore not over whether we seek the Lord. It is over *why* we come to seek the Lord if we do. Men, left to themselves, will not seek God. And this is what the Bible explicitly teaches. How many are unrighteous? All. How many seek a way out of their unrighteousness? None:

> As it is written: "There is none righteous, no, not one; There is none who understands; There is none who seeks after God. They have all turned aside; They have together become unprofitable; There is none who does good, no, not one." (Rom. 3:10–12)

The nonbeliever is trapped by an essential hostility of mind to the things of God—"Because the carnal mind is enmity against God; for it is not subject to the law of God, nor indeed can be. So then, those who are in the flesh cannot please God" (Rom. 8:7–8; cf. 1 Cor. 2:14).

So who then can be saved? The problem with all this is that it leaves us without hope of salvation, right? No, it leaves us without hope of salvation from *man*. What is impossible for men is possible for God: "No one can come to Me unless the Father who sent Me draws him; and I will raise him up at the last day" (John 6:44; cf. v. 65).

If the Father does not do the drawing, if the Father does not give it, then a man cannot come. But does this mean that no one ever comes? No—it means that everyone who comes has been drawn by God. And further, when the Father draws, that drawing is inexorable: "All that the

Father gives Me will come to Me, and the one who comes to Me I will by no means cast out" (John 6:37). What man cannot do with any success, God can do with no failure. And what is that? The resurrection of the dead. A man who could repent and believe with his old heart didn't really need a new one.

So we know that God does this for those He determines to save. But when did He make this determination? This brings us to the subject of election. We must begin with the understanding that election cannot be understood apart from Christ. Christ is the Elect One, and all those whom God chose to give to Him are therefore elect in *Him*: "Behold! My Servant whom I uphold, My Elect One in whom My soul delights! I have put My Spirit upon Him; He will bring forth justice to the Gentiles" (Is. 42:1). The New Testament contains this same truth and points to Christ as the Elect of God—"Therefore it is also contained in the Scripture, 'Behold, I lay in Zion a chief cornerstone, elect, precious, and he who believes on Him will by no means be put to shame'" (1 Peter 2:6). Peter also points to this truth earlier, when he says, "He indeed was foreordained before the foundation of the world, but was manifest in these last times for you . . ." (1 Peter 1:20).

But Christ is not the only one who is elect. Our election and Christ's election are seen together—"Father, I desire that they also whom You gave Me may be with Me where I am, that they may behold My glory which You have given Me; for You loved Me before the foundation of the world" (John 17:24).

When did this election take place? The biblical answer to this question is unambiguous. Before the world was created, before eternal times, God picked out a people for Himself. For those who seek to honor Scripture, there can be no real debate about when God's election of His people occurred—"who has saved us and called us with a holy calling, not according to our works, but according to His own purpose and grace which was given to us in Christ Jesus *before time began*" (2 Tim. 1:9). Two more should suffice: "Then the King will say to those on His right hand, 'Come, you blessed of My Father, inherit the kingdom prepared for you *from the foundation of the world*'" (Matt. 25:34). And of course Paul encourages us this way—"just as He chose us in Him *before the foundation of the world*, that we should be holy and without blame before Him in love" (Eph. 1:4).

Why? For those who believe the Bible, this is really the heart of the debate. There is really no honest way to evade the force of the Bible's teaching on *when* election occurs. Therefore, those who dispute this truth do it by seeking to modify the *nature* of this election. The biblical position is that God made this choice according to His good pleasure. The more popular view is that He made His choice on account of foreseen faith.

But the Bible excludes human choices as the basis of God's choice:

> For the children not yet being born, nor having done any good or evil, that the purpose of God according to election might stand, not of works but of Him who calls. . . . So then it is *not of him who wills*, nor of him who runs, but of God who shows mercy. . . . Therefore He has mercy on whom He wills, and whom He wills He hardens. (Rom. 9:11, 16, 18)

But what about those passages which seem to talk about God's foreknowledge as the basis of His choice? Peter refers to the "elect according to the foreknowledge of God the Father, in sanctification of the Spirit, for obedience and sprinkling of the blood of Jesus Christ: Grace to you and peace be multiplied" (1 Pet. 1:2). And Paul says, "For whom He foreknew, He also predestined to be conformed to the image of His Son, that He might be the firstborn among many brethren" (Rom. 8:29).

In Peter, it simply says that election is in accordance with foreknowledge; it says nothing about God choosing based upon His foreknowledge of our choices. And there are two important things to note in the Romans passage. One is the object of the verb, and the second is the nature of the verb. The object consists of persons, not actions—those *whom* He foreknew. And so the verb refers to love, not cognition of certain choices. Before the world was created, God knew us and loved us.

The Reformed view of Christ's atonement is obviously affected by all of this. This understanding is that Christ died to secure the salvation of all God's elect. But before discussing this, we must begin by rejecting a term that is commonly applied to this doctrine.

The rejected term is that of limited atonement, which should be rejected for two reasons. One is that it is misleading with regard to the teaching of the Bible, and the other is that it misrepresents the debate. One of the most obvious features of the atonement in Scripture is its *universality*. Consequently, a phrase which appears to deny that universality on the surface is not useful. Secondly, every Christian who holds to the reality of eternal judgment believes (in some sense) in a limited atonement. The debate is over what aspect is limited—efficacy or extent.

Present the question to yourself in this way. It is not a choice between limited and unlimited atonement. It is a choice between definite and indefinite atonement. It is a choice between an effectual redemption and an ineffectual redemption.

As evangelical Christians, we believe in a vicarious atonement. The universality of the atonement in Scripture is not the only obvious thing about it. Another truth, equally precious and equally clear, is that the atonement is *substitutionary*. This means that if Christ died for someone, the "for" means "instead of." It is not a potential substitution: "if . . ." It is an actual substitution and therefore efficacious (2 Cor. 5:21; 1 Pet. 3:18)—"I am the good shepherd; and I know My sheep, and am known by My own. As the Father knows Me, even so I know the Father; and *I lay down My life for the sheep*" (John 10:14–15). Jesus plainly tells us that He died for His sheep. A few verses later, He makes a very interesting limitation: "Jesus answered them, 'I told you, and you do not believe. The works that I do in My Father's name, they bear witness of Me. But you do not believe, because *you are not of My sheep*, as I said to you. My sheep hear My voice, and I know them, and they follow Me'" (John 10:25–27). The Lord tells us that He lays down His life for the sheep, and then He tells us that certain individuals are *not* His sheep. Further, He says they do not believe because they are not His sheep. He does not say they are not His sheep because they do not believe.

The debate centers on the meaning of the word *for* in the phrase, "Jesus died for sinners." One position is that Jesus died *to give a chance to* sinners. The position I believe to be more biblical is that Jesus died *instead of* sinners.

God's sovereignty is also obvious at the point of conversion. We have seen that the condition of man is such that he cannot save himself or contribute to his own salvation. Secondly, we have read that the Father elected some to salvation before the creation of the world. Election is the work of the Father. Outside Jerusalem two thousand years ago, the Son of God secured the salvation of His people on the cross. Efficacious redemption is the work of the Son. And now we will see that in our salvation, the Father, Son, and Holy Spirit are all working in the same direction.

What happens in the lives of individuals when they are born again? This is the work of the Spirit, which we may refer to as the effectual or resurrecting call.

Now the Bible does use the word call in at least three different ways. We need not spend a lot of time on the first use; it is simply a synonym for *named*: "And Jacob begot Joseph the husband of Mary, of whom was born Jesus who is called Christ" (Matt. 1:16).

But the second and third usages are often confused in the minds of Christians, so we must spend more time on them. We have to recognize a general or indiscriminate call to all men. The Bible uses the word *call* or *called* in the sense of *invite* or *invited*. In other words, the one invited can take the invitation or leave it: "When He had called the multitude to Himself, He said to them, 'Hear and understand . . .'" (Matt. 15:10). In this passage, Jesus is simply inviting men to hear what He has to say. There is no indication of any special power or authority in the invitation. There is even a passage where the word is used in this general way with regard to salvation: "For many are called, but few are chosen" (Matt. 22:14). We can see that this call is not efficacious because it is set in contrast with God's choice, which *is* efficacious. So the word *called* may legitimately be used in a general, indiscriminate way. There are many of those who are not elect who do hear the gospel invitation—it falls on their ears. And in this external way, they are invited. But because of the sinfulness of their hearts, they will not respond to the invitation. Unless God issues an effectual call.

The Bible also—very clearly—uses the word *called* as a label for those who are believers, in contrast with those who are unbelievers. In other words, there is a saving call that is not extended to every last person. For example:

> And we know that all things work together for good to those who love God, to *those who are the called* according to His purpose. . . . Moreover whom He predestined, *these He also called;* whom He *called,* these He also justified; and whom He justified, these He also glorified. (Rom. 8:28, 30)

In another place, Paul speaks in the same way—

> For Jews request a sign, and Greeks seek after wisdom; but we preach Christ crucified, to the Jews a stumbling block and to the Greeks foolishness, *but to those*

who are called, both Jews and Greeks, Christ the power
of God and the wisdom of God. (1 Cor. 1:22–24; cf.
2 Tim. 1:9)

In these passages, we see that effectual calling is se-
curely linked to God's predestined purpose beforehand,
our final glorification, and an understanding of the cross.
It is *not* based upon our receptivity to the cross—rather,
our receptivity to the cross is based upon it. Nor is it based
on our works—in any way, shape, or form.

As a result, we live our lives confident that God will
finish in us what He started. This aspect of the Reformed
view of salvation is called the perseverance of the saints.
This is the one aspect of all this that the natural man thinks
he might be able to like. But like all spiritual truth, the
natural man can only love the truth through a distortion
of it.

The question is not whether Christians can lose salvation—as though salvation were a possession of *ours,* like
car keys or something. The real question is whether Christ
can lose a Christian or not. The Bible teaches us that salvation means that we are a possession of *His.*

Man-centeredness causes some to talk about this as
though it were a mere reversal of regeneration. "This man
was once regenerate but now he isn't anymore." But when
salvation is understood biblically, that is, as rooted in the
eternal will of the Father in election, in the eternal blood
of the covenant that secured their salvation, and in the
resurrection of the Spirit bringing them into life, the idea
of a man losing his salvation means that God's words must
fall to the ground.

Man is mutable and what he does can be undone, but
God is immutable and what He determines cannot be undone. There are many passages which assert this, but one
of the clearest is found in Romans 8, which has to be
quoted at length:

And we know that all things work together for good to those who love God, to those who are the called according to His purpose. For whom He foreknew, He also predestined to be conformed to the image of His Son, that He might be the firstborn among many brethren. Moreover whom He predestined, these He also called; whom He called, these He also justified; and whom He justified, these He also glorified. *What then shall we say to these things?* If God is for us, who can be against us? He who did not spare His own Son, but delivered Him up for us all, how shall He not with Him also freely give us all things? *Who shall bring a charge against God's elect?* It is God who justifies. Who is he who condemns? It is Christ who died, and furthermore is also risen, who is even at the right hand of God, who also makes intercession for us. Who shall separate us from the love of Christ? Shall tribulation, or distress, or persecution, or famine, or nakedness, or peril, or sword? As it is written: "For Your sake we are killed all day long; We are accounted as sheep for the slaughter." Yet in all these things we are more than conquerors through Him who loved us. *For I am persuaded* that neither death nor life, nor angels nor principalities nor powers, nor things present nor things to come, nor height nor depth, nor any other created thing, shall be able to separate us from the love of God which is in Christ Jesus our Lord. (Rom. 8:28–39)

So we have finished our sketch of Reformed doctrine. Why does it matter in classical Christian schools? And how should we conduct ourselves in the midst of disagreements on this subject? Let us begin with the second question first.

Unity and Doctrine

This is an important issue to settle in our minds. It is obvious that this is not a dispute about lesser matters like baptism or church government. For those who have followed closely, this whole debate really centers on the meaning of the gospel. How should we then approach brothers in the Lord who differ with us on this subject? How may differences be accomodated within a school if they are differences on the nature of the *gospel*?

The first thing to address is attitude:

> And a servant of the Lord must not quarrel but be gentle to all, able to teach, patient, in humility correcting those who are in opposition, if God perhaps will grant them repentance, so that they may know the truth, and that they may come to their senses and escape the snare of the devil, having been taken captive by him to do his will. (2 Tim. 2:24–26)

Controversy is sometimes unavoidable, but we should always seek to conduct ourselves in the midst of it with the attitude Paul requires here—gentle to all and humble.

In this same passage, note the application of "Reformed theology." The verse says that *God* is the one who grants repentance. Now do we use this as a prooftext to beat over the head those who deny it? Or do we do what the verse says to do? Put another way, how can we expect others to affirm with their lips what we deny with our attitudes?

We then come to the question of the distinctions we must make. There are several tasks that Christian leaders have which require a large measure of discrimination. The Bible requires elders, for example, to be able to refute false teachers: "Holding fast the faithful word as he has been taught, that he may be able, by sound doctrine, both to exhort and convict those who contradict" (Titus 1:9). But at the same time, the leaders are required to be able to instruct and encourage the weak, the confused, the "lied to," and so forth. This means that an important distinction must be made and maintained between those who are confused about sound doctrine and those who hate it. And even with those who hate it, we must ber the earlier passage that requires a real gentleness in refutation.

It is my conviction that evangelical Christians hold to the basics of the gospel, although I believe them to be confused about some aspects of it. This is a very different thing than promoting a false gospel.

So the school is not a place where we set aside our convictions about the sovereignty of God. It is one of the best places to begin applying our convictions about the sovereignty of God. Because God is sovereign, we confess that we do not see into hearts and should not act as though we do. If some profess Christ as Lord and are not characterized by immorality or active opposition to the gospel, then we should fellowship with them and seek to work together with them. Working with them must include educating our children together. We must also confess that we do not determine the boundaries of salvation—*God* does. We must follow His lead and must not seek to have higher fellowship standards than He does. For example, did God fellowship with you and have communion with you before you understood these truths? Salvation is based on the truth of Romans 9, not our complete understanding of Romans 9. Because we are saved by sovereign grace, Arminians are saved for the same reason that Calvinists who are inconsistent in some *other* area are saved.

The Point of All This

This discussion may have seemed to come at the question before us in a very roundabout way. Why a survey of the history of the doctrinal controversy, and why a sketch of the heart of Reformed thinking? We can perhaps see why the section just before this might be important; we know that we are dealing with disagreements, and the unity of the saints must always be carefully tended. But why all this other stuff?

First, it is simply a fact that many classical Christian schools are Reformed in their doctrinal outlook. Others, which are not explicitly Reformed, have found themselves attracting a great deal of Reformed support. In dealing with this, we must take care that we deal with the doctrines as they are held and not with caricatures of those doctrines. Ignorance coupled with good wishes will never advance the unity of the saints. In Scripture, unity is always around the *truth*, and not around sentiment, or a *verboten* subject.

Secondly, now that we have considered the outlines of Reformed theology, we should be able to see why classical and Christian schools are so attractive to the Reformed. The classical Christian school movement emphasizes the integration of all subject matter with the Scriptures at the center. Because the Reformed believe that God is involved in *everything*, this is also a classical school emphasis. And on the contrary side, the modern evangelical notion that there are various aspects of life with which God has nothing to do makes it difficult (and I would argue, impossible) for them to develop an integrated Christian worldview. This means that the modern evangelical mindset is distinctively uncongenial to the classical mindset. Because classical Christian schools insist on educating with a full-orbed biblical worldview, and because the Reformed emphasize the same thing (for theological reasons), cooperation between the two becomes essential.

Third, the classical Christian school movement also emphasizes a return to the careful study of the history of our people. As the historical sketch earlier in this essay should have made clear, Reformed theology of some kind or other has been a major factor in the history of ideas. John Calvin's *Institutes of the Christian Religion* is one of the most influential books ever written. And we have to confess that Augustine of Hippo was the most influential man who has lived since the time of the apostles. With our classical understanding of history, we may not avoid the ideas that threw numerous centuries into turmoil simply because we may find them personally inconvenient. History happened the way it did, and if we simply squint at it all from a safe distance, we are in fact repudiating the profession of teaching. Men who were Reformed and who were shaped and driven by that doctrine include John Calvin, Stonewall Jackson, William of Orange, William Tyndale, John Wyclif, John Knox, John Witherspoon, and countless others whose names the reader would immediately recognize. Without a clear understanding of Reformed theology, we cannot understand much of our history at all.

Part of the reason the Reformed have been so influential *in* history is that they have such a strong doctrine *of* history. This in turn is because they have a strong doctrine of the providence of God over all history. And without that doctrine of providence, the whole thing starts to unravel. Our understanding of ourselves as a people has unraveled; this is part of the reason why classical and Christian schools have met with such success. People are tired of superficial, pietistic, easy answers. It is time for the hard questions and time for our children to face the hard questions.

Fourth, many of those who are involved in starting up classical and Christian schools are on their own pilgrimage. They do not have any settled doctrinal convictions but are unsettled by that fact. They feel rootless and unequipped to teach their children. They have begun the process regardless, and they have constantly come up against what may be described as a fundamental theological reason why their studies seem so fruitless. They are trying to be faithful but cannot seem to get any traction. I have seen numerous such individuals who have begun to investigate Reformed theology precisely because their previous theology (or, more likely, lack of theology) provided an inadequate foundation for the kind of education they wanted to provide for their children.

And lastly, a word to those faithful Christian and classical educators who for various reasons (pervasive to them) are not Reformed: My point here has been that there is a *reason* why Reformed theology and classical Christian education go so well together and that in the convergence of the two we are seeing more than just a coincidence. The objective here has not been to introduce unnecessary strife but to show that the success of the classical Christian school movement depends upon it being, as was said earlier, either Reformed or congenial to Reformed theology. In short, the only way the classical and Christian school movement could possibly get the Reformed to go away would be through abandoning all the disinctives of the classical and Christian approach to education.

This brings difficulties with it because Reformed theology is controversial in many quarters, and a school struggling to build a successful program may feel it is unwise to meddle in unnecessary issues or controversies. The Reformed bring many resources, but they also bring controversy in their train. This is because some of them are cranky, but basically it is because the Reformed cast of mind is very different from that applauded by modernity. Is there a way around this? Unfortunately, if the history of the Church over the last seventeen hundred years is any indication, the answer is *no*. But when controversy arises, we can resolve to be good stewards of it and strive for unity in the truth and likemindedness as the apostle requires.

At all costs, a classical and Christian school must not attempt to get along by *suppressing* issues. To succeed that way is to fail.

Chapter Six:

The Great Logic Fraud

A Somber Exordium

One unhappy result of this essay on logic and mathematical epistemology, not to mention various points of grammar, will probably be a ganglion of grievous misunderstandings. I am afraid that nothing can be done about this other than to anticipate the problem and to try to be winsome in the first paragraph. There.

High standards in education are regarded by modern educrats with great suspicion, and so it is not surprising that in the return to classical and Christian education, many are calling for a return to rigorous and serious education, with strict and *defined* standards. I have been among those agitating for such a return, and nothing in these essays should be taken as a reversal of this desire.

At the same time, we must exercise great care. Logic, rightly understood, is an attribute of God. But many things have been done in the name of logic and mathematical abstractions that, as distortions of an important truth, misrepresent the nature of God more than anything else. And something similar happens with the perfectionism that afflicts many prescriptivist grammarians. Unless we are careful, the return to classical education will be diverted into an earlier, rigorist form of modernism. This will not represent true educational reform; rather it will be just the next sorry chapter of the perennial teetertottering of

Apollonians and Dionysians, going up and down, up and down.

The applicability of this essay (and the next one) for classical educators may not seem immediately obvious, but they are particularly intended for those involved in the work of establishing and maintaining schools which follow the trivium, with particular attention being paid here to the dialectical stage, or the logic stage. This is intended not to alter what is being taught at this level but to alter how some are tempted to *think* about this level. The subjects addressed here are simply enormous, and no attempt has been made to address and answer all the questions. The design has been simply to be provocative and to call us to remember our priorities. We need to be constantly reminded that logic and grammar are the preparation for the last level of the trivium, that of rhetoric, the level where young men and women come to maturity, growing up to the level of understanding *poetry*.

And Now, A Chatty Exordium

I must begin with an unusual disclaimer, or at least unusual coming from one who would like to convince his readers of anything. H.L. Mencken once defined self-respect as that deep, self-assured feeling that no one, as of yet, is suspicious. In the pages that follow, learned readers may want to conclude that the time has come for the present writer to relinquish all pretenses to such self-respect, at least on the subject that was occupying him at the time of writing.

This is because I cannot claim to be any good at mathematical-like endeavors. Further, despite having co-authored a book on symbolic logic, I cannot claim to be any good at that either. All the precision of mind evident in that most valuable work was the contribution of the other guy. For various reasons, many of them very sad, my mind does not work the way a logic teacher's mind ought to work. My mastery of the holy mysteries of theoretical physics is laughable. I took a geometry class in high school, which was kind of fun, but an unsatiable appetite for more was not exactly whetted during that time.

But enough with the autobiographical lament. The reason I had to begin with this expression of extraordinary humility and self-abasement, every word of it true, is that the following essay is going to seem to many, especially those who are trained in propositional and predicate logic, mathematics, syntactical linguistics, or physics, as being extraordinarily arrogant. And this is because, despite all my protests above, it will become rapidly apparent that I am treating my ignorance as one of my primary qualifications for addressing this subject. Having confessed my ignorance, it will soon appear that I am insufficiently ashamed and abased.

But a man doesn't have to know how to drive in order to form a justified, true belief that the fellow up in the front seat, who *does* know to drive, has gotten himself onto the wrong road. In fact, not having to drive gives that fellow some time to muse, gazing out the back window, wondering why the scenery looks so funny.

Disciplines sometimes overlap, and this causes no end of confusion and misapplication. Someone who plays second base for the Yankees or Braves becomes a national advertising authority on shaving cream. Carl Sagan pronounces on things he never saw through a telescope. A mathematician orders three eggs and the cook serves up two of them, and the mathematician rightly believes he has the authority to object. So sometimes the overlap results in areas of joint expertise, and sometimes it results in a fellow speaking to areas where he has no expertise.

Many of the problems we have in understanding how rationalistic abstractions (like mathematics and symbolic logic) relate to the world are theological and philosophical. This is often missed because those who have competence to address the theological or philosophical ramifications of some of these issues are airily dismissed because they may lack higher mathematical competence. And yet, if disciplines overlap, perhaps this grants them some perspective. Perhaps someone off to the side may be able to point out that a form of Platonism, formally rejected in many areas, retains supremacy in the realm of mathematical logic, and hence it is the great surreptitious philosophy of the twentieth century.

At the heart of this Hellenistic framework is the practice of granting an autonomous ontological status to the realm of abstractions. In the area of mathematics and many other realms directly affected by mathematical assumptions, this essential Platonism remains unchallenged. This problem is going to be referred to so many times throughout this essay that I have coined a word to describe it— to *ontize* means to assume that something has some sort of ontological status simply because the conceptual framework for it is self-consistent, or put another way, simply because the math works.

A brief review of the history of ideas on our planet should show that smart people have generally been able to say pretty much anything they have wanted to. But nimbleness of wit does not always function as wisdom, and the fact that the boys down at the body and fender shop cannot see through the mathematical smoke screen does not mean the impressive display means anything.

Several other comments are necessary. First, it will become clear I have assumed that the reader is familar with certain issues in philosophy and logic, and with some of the terms and notation that come with those issues. While I have sought to use such things to make the point, I have also endeavored to write around them so that the general reader can still follow the argument. This said, I do not want any readers unfamiliar with the language or notation to be buffaloed by my use of it. Anyone who *is* familiar with these things is almost certainly more familiar with them than am I, and anything that looks impressive, or like some weird alchemic thoughtform, was done laboriously and with great care, with the present writer's tongue sticking out the side of his mouth.

Secondly, the issues brought up here—math, relativity, dictionaries, etc.—may seem to be little more than an exercise in randomness. But a central point ties them all together, which is that rationalism is not rationality, and the rigid imposition of arbitrary and abstract standards is not the same thing as returning to a classical pattern of education. In the life of the modern mind, a number of apparently unrelated areas are connected by a hidden Cartesian rationalism; the intention here is simply to point to those areas and make some assertions in the hope of beginning a fruitful discussion, particularly among educators. Detailed proof will have to await the publication of a multi-volume series by somebody.

Seduced by All Those Shapely Forms

The Platonic temptation is a persistent one. In the Middle Ages, Christian thinkers began to shake off their philosophical realism inherited from the Greeks and began to work through the ramifications of a more consistently Christian nominalism. But Western culture needed more time in the detox center than was actually spent there, and the temptation to go back to realist assumptions has been constant and unrelenting. This has been particularly the case with mathematics and its cousins—theoretical physics and symbolic logic in particular. Many modern fads and fashions—the fruitless attempts to create artificial intelligence, say—continue to exert a spell entirely on the strength of an underlying and invisible Platonism.

The nominalism of William of Ockham was generally Augustinian, and so the realm of particular things was tied together in the predestination of God—whether or not his Augustinianism was weak or strong. Thus a hedgehog and a pair of scissors inhabited the same universe, a universe under the Lordship of Christ. But when that faith in the predestination or foreknowledge of God lost its *arche*, nominalism drifted off into the skepticism of David Hume, who looked first at this thing and then at that and realized that, absent heaven, he had no earthly way to tie the two things together. Jean-Paul Sartre once correctly observed that, without an infinite reference point, every finite point is absurd.

The moral of the story is not that nominalism has been tried and found wanting but that unless nominalism remains trinitarian and Augustinian it will float off into a vision of the world that looks something like a music video by Peter Gabriel. But following the way of all flesh, nominalism slipped away from this necessary *arche,* for it was assumed by many to be a non starter, and the philosophical world drifted back to a form of realism again. One distinctive feature of this is that many moderns appear not to know that these enormous shifts have even happened.

Now Plato believed in the transcendent realm of the Forms. In order to make sense of three oranges, or three philosophers for that matter, he appealed to that realm where Threeness held its abode. Thus he was able (at least he thought) to keep the oranges and the philosophers in the same world. He believed that such a transcendent abode was *really there*, and moreover, that it was more real than the shadowy realm where we pass our shadowy lives. Further, this shadowy realm took the form it did because of what was in the realm of the Forms.

Now the point of this essay is not to argue that modern mathematicians believe that the square of the hypotenuse lives in Heaven but to argue that something much more subtle has occurred. The names certainly have been changed; we no longer speak of the realm of the Forms. We do, however, speak quite freely of the various "dimensions" beyond the ones we experience, and in addition, we moderns treat our abstractions as though they in some way *exist*. But no one has seen—or could see—the tenth dimension, where some physicists postulate the vibrating of superstring, whose vibrations supposedly bring everything into existence. "The ideer! Tell us more, perfesser!"

Rather, my point here is that such speculations—and all speculations like it—are at bottom indistinguishable from the ancient Platonic mindset. In this respect, the rationalism of modernist logic, mathematics, and various forms of scientism are all Plato *redivivus*. Because the adoption of these Hellenistic assumptions has been virtually universal in some of our mathematical assumptions, they are equally invisible to us all. But we should all come to realize that a medieval nominalist would look agog at some of our processes of thought. So, while some of the comments that follow may initially seem somewhat rude or unlettered, the problem is that we have not yet brought the insights of a Christian nominalism to the realm of mathematics and its cousins.

And in bringing such a nominalistic framework to bear on this problem, I am not seeking to make my point in the way that modern realists want to require me to make it. A refusal to play on *that* turf is part of *this* game.

Three Is an Adjective

Everyone knows that blue and yellow make green. Well, actually blue paint and yellow paint make green paint, and blue light and yellow light make green light. Nevertheless, we still want to say, using an abstraction as a form of shorthand, that blue and yellow make green. But in the real world, the world God made, blue and yellow do not exist independently of the nouns they modify. It is true that blue and green can be considered as abstract nouns, and that is fine as far as it goes. Abstractions like truth, beauty, and green are necessary in order for us to communicate at all. But we must be careful here because our entire problem rests in what we have thought we are allowed to do with abstractions.

This lack of "existence" is true of all adjectives, including those adjectives we call numbers. One, three, and seven do not exist independently of the nouns they modify—e.g., one truck, three beers, or the seven churches of the province of Asia.

It follows from this that addition occurs in the world God made, and multiplication does *not* so occur. Two eggs can be added to one egg, making three in all. But in the world we live in, the world of clouds and rain, earth and sky, gravel driveways and cars that go, multiplication never occurs—only addition. Division never occurs, only subtraction. What we call multiplication is nothing but *a mental shortcut* that enables us to calculate the results of the more time-consuming and laborious addition. If someone is told that the auditorium has twenty rows of seats, with fifteen seats in a row, he can calculate the number of seats in the auditorium quickly without counting each seat. The number of seats is three hundred, but this can be confirmed only by adding them up. But when someone assumes that multiplication exists in the world or in a world of its own, then the multiplication table has been ontized.

Numbers do not exist on their own. If I add one apple to another apple the result is that I have two apples. By the same token, if I add a green apple to a red apple I get exactly the same result—two apples. Numbers are only adjectives, descriptive of those things that exist in the world God made. They have names, and because we intend to call them by their names, we are nominalists. These adjectives do not stand alone in some realm of the Forms or in any realm or dimension *like* the realm of the Forms. Using one as an abstract noun is fine, as long as we do not forget ourselves and begin thinking of it as having its own free-standing reality.

We may be helped in this by borrowing an essential distinction from formal logic, the distinction between truth and validity. Validity refers to structural soundness while truth refers to conformity with the external world. In part, we must learn to think the same way about our math problems. For example, the argument that follows is called *modus ponens*, or "way of affirming," and is valid. This means that the conclusion is necessarily true if it is assumed for the sake of argument that the premises are true. Validity has to do with structure, and when we have all that we need to know about the structure of the argument, we can pronounce it valid, whether or not we know *what* is being said. The premises may or may not be true. But if they are, then the conclusion must necessarily be true because the argument is structurally sound.

If *P* then *Q*
P
Therefore, *Q*

But we do not yet know whether the premises are true, and thus we do not know if the conclusion is true. This is because we do not yet know what we will insert for *P* and *Q*. If we insert various falsehoods or nullities, the argument remains valid because its structure is sound. We can know that the structure is sound even when we haven't said anything yet.

Now bring this to mathematics. Because of our realist assumptions in mathematics, we have come to believe that $15 + 20 = 35$ is *true*. But it is evidently not true. 15 unicorns plus 20 unicorns will not get you 35 unicorns, try as you may. Of course, on the other hand, 15 turnips plus 20 turnips will result in 35 turnips, and it will do so every time. The structure of the addition table is sound, and the "argument" is valid. And if unicorns existed, we would wind up with 35 of them. But this means the argument is valid, not true.

In mathematics when we say $15x$, the *x* stands in for an unknown number, and the 15 is multiplied with that number. But we also need a notation, at least when we are making this point, in which a separate symbol stands in for a *noun*. In what follows, I have somewhat arbitrarily chosen the letter *beta*.

Using this notation the same basic way as we do in logic can be helpful in making this point. Thus no difference exists between $15 + 20 = 35$ and $15\beta + 20\beta = 35\beta$. Because we do not know what noun is represented by β, we do not know whether the solution to our problem is true. But it is valid in a way that $15\beta + 20\beta = 3\beta$ is not valid.

What does all this mean? Just that there is no realm where numbers and their functions live.

Many Dimensions

Another place where our Platonic realism still affects us is in our thinking about space and time. We commonly speak of three-dimensional space, that space consisting of height, breadth, and depth. In relativity theory a fourth dimension is added, and then that of time makes five dimensions. But some of the assumptions made in this are breathtaking. How is it, for example, that height and time have been shown to belong to the same genus, that of "dimension," and how has it been shown that we can add them together? Further, if we consider the work of theoretical physicists, where did we get our apparently inexhaustible supply of new dimensions, and how did we discover that they can be added to each other just like the first five can be? The reasons are that *we can make the math work* and that we sometimes see things in the empirical realm that are consistent with that math. But such consistency, while received with loud hurrahs by people hungry for "scientific" proofs, does not constitute proof.

What we have done is grant ontological (realist) status to any abstraction or adjectival description we may happen to make. *We ontize that description.* Although we no longer locate this realm in the Heavens, we still behave as though we have located it *somewhere* special. Somewhere, somehow, there are these things called dimensions, which can be stacked on top of one another as though they were building blocks. Thus, theoretical physicists have broad scope for their speculations and may step high, wide, and plentiful up to the chalkboard. If we have five dimensions, then why not six? Ten? Twenty-two? We continue to speak long after our words have any conceivable meaning.

In the face of this, more traditional physicists have sought to keep their discipline from becoming little more than a branch of aesthetics by insisting that some sort of experimental verification be required. Thus some of the more speculative theories in physics have been rejected. But the verification accepted has been that of being able to make predictions, which is not necessarily the same thing as proof.

For example, if a man's theory is that some animal off in the distance is a cow, he might predict that the animal would have four legs, and any discovery that it does have four legs would be consistent with the thesis. But what if it has four legs because it is an elk? Put another way, what serves as empirical verification in much speculative science is nothing other than the old fallacy of affirming the consequent. The symbolic form of this is:

If P then Q
Q
Therefore, P

A chain of these may make a strong inductive argument, but they do *not* constitute proof, especially in those areas on the outer cosmic frontiers of the whole relativity shebang.

To illustrate the problem with this, take the common example of relativity being verified—that of atomic clocks running at different rates in different planes, showing that movement affects time. Or take the experiments in which atomic clocks run at different rates when on the top of a mountain and down at sea level, ostensibly showing that gravity has an effect on time. The empirical differences are certainly there, but this could be accounted for by any number of things.

Far from showing that time is relative, this may just be showing that *clocks* are relative. But of course in relativity a philosophical assumption is made which equates time with the clocks. Time does not exist apart from clocks. But that is a philosophical question, not an experimental one. To oversimplify the problem, could we prove that time moves more slowly in a bucket of syrup by dropping an alarm clock into it?

We need to back up. Space is simply one "dimension," with three distinguishable but inseparable attributes. If the height of my laptop computer were removed, the breadth and length of it would not remain. We have no reason to believe that any of these attributes can be subtracted from the whole, and the same goes for adding them. But the common Platonic notion is that each dimension has independent existence, each one having been ontized, and that when they come together we have the thing we call space. This means they can be taken apart and retain their independent existence, or they can be multiplied and have a mysterious hyper-dimensional existence. The fact that no one can conceptualize, or describe, or define, or explain these dimensions *without resorting to mathematics* should make the thoughtful observer pause. When pondering imponderables, with scads of arbitrary variables, we should acknowledge that the likelihood of error is, well . . . high.

A Non-Euclidean of a Different Color

When we are solving geometric problems, we resort to an elegant kind of abstraction. In order to work with the proof, we want to use a mental chalkboard that remains entirely free of mental "chalkdust." Thus, when a straight line crosses two parallel lines at an angle, we want to say the acute angles formed at the point of intersection on the corresponding sides of each line are both the same. But we want to calculate this without making our problem more complicated than necessary. This means we do not want to have to mess with how thick the lines are. So we don't. In this handy *and very imaginary* world, the lines have no thickness at all. Points have no length, and squares have no height.

In this imaginary, mental-chalkboard world of ours, it makes sense to speak of one-dimensional, two-dimensional, and three-dimensional space, but only because we are using an abstraction, a mental shortcut. This is all well and good, and perfectly necessary if we are to get anything done. The problem arises when Platonism does—that is, when we assume that this "flatland" we have been thinking about actually exists somehow, somewhere.

This world of abstractions is assumed to have authority over the world that actually exists when someone argues, as Zeno once did, that motion is impossible. In order to go a particular distance, one would have to go half the distance first. In order to go that distance, one would have to go halfway, and so on. Thus, it is impossible for anyone to move, because each movement must be preceded by a movement halfway. But this argument depends upon the notion that a finite line in the world God made is infinitely divisible simply because a finite line is infinitely divisible in the world Euclid made. A child's ball might go bouncing by us, but we philosophers can dismiss it as an illusion because we understand the math.

But Reality Intrudes

We run into trouble in symbolic logic as well. The assumption is made (accurately) that we may develop an algebra of thought. We may analyze arguments by studying their raw structural form. That is, we may substitute Ps and Qs and Rs for the various claims made in an argument. Thus the premise that if a man studies hard he will grow in knowledge, coupled with the fact that he has in fact studied hard, results in the necessary conclusion that he will grow in knowledge. The form of this hypothetical syllogism was referred to above and is called *modus ponens*.

But if these things are not closely watched, they get away from us, and we will forget the necessary limitations in all such reductions. The structural argument is always valid, everything else being equal, but in the messy world, everything else is rarely equal. This bare bones structure is ontized and then is assumed to have authority over real-world situations and arguments. The results are sometimes curious and sometimes funny.

We all know that a good course in logic will help a student to stop arguing that wet streets cause rain. But the temptation to ontize is always great. For example, logicians have developed a powerful tool that helps them analyze many arguments. The use of truth functional analysis and truth tables provides a very helpful way of examing arguments. However, in the world of truth functions, the statements *if P then Q* and *not P or Q* are considered equivalent. In most cases this is all very well and good, and very helpful. But in a few places, difficulties arise.

For example, it enables us to argue:

1. Pigs are not bright green. [not P]
2. Therefore, pigs are not bright green or the pope is the mayor of Buffalo. [not P or Q]
3. Therefore, if pigs were bright green, the pope would be the mayor of Buffalo. [if P then Q]

The form of this would be:

1. $\sim P$
2. $\sim P \lor Q$
3. $P \supset Q$

In the world of our symbols, this is valid all the way down the line. But in the world of English, or any other spoken language, it is not valid. Further, the pristine logical form misrepresents the created world as it is. Clearly this means there is some problem; this illustrates how our logical symbols have certain limitations, and all such symbolic reductions are at some level reductionistic.

This should have been expected, because logical notation is another language, and in *all* translations, *something is lost*. In German, the dividing line between *warm* and *hot* is different than it is in English. In Greek, the dividing line between *tree* and *bush* is different than it is in English. In symbolic notation, precision of meaning is key, with every element in the proposition having a denotation and no connotations. In a spoken language, connotations are inescapable. Thus symbolic notation of a spoken argument can be quite helpful, but that notation is not exhaustive, and it does not translate everything that is there. Precise notation is rigid, and consequently it is sometimes brittle.

Nothing can be done about this, and nobody should try. Of necessity, all translations alter the words; we cannot keep what we have—*quoad verbum*. But a good translation can approximate the meaning—*quoad res*. Thus *Claudius feminam amavit* means that Claudius loved a woman. The words are altered, but the meaning remains essentially the same. But if I were to render it "Herbert loves fly-fishing," then the translation would be a bad one—*quoad res*.

But even good translations have limitations with regard to the matter. If I were to translate *Claudius feminam amat*, this could be rendered at least three ways. Latin has only one form of the present tense while English has three. Thus an English speaker could "nuance" this as it pleased him. Claudius loves, or Claudius is loving, or Claudius does love a woman. And, as we shall see coming up, this is just a mild example of the translation woes that can come from a simple three word sentence.

As we have noted, when dealing with logical notation, precision of meaning is key. But in order to get this precision, we must alter how words such as *or* work, and this means that we can come up with absurdities like the color of pigs dictating whether the pope will stand for office in upstate New York. No translation, *including translation into symbolic notation*, can escape the cliché that every translation "loses something in translation." In its native habitat, every argument has a suppleness it cannot have elsewhere. To be sure, translation into logical notation can reveal that somebody was arguing some absurdity in English, and this is where such notation is helpful. But this does not mean that the notation is in any sense the ideal—or the most accurate—language. However, many of those attracted to proficiency in symbolic notation do not seem to understand this. They think that their reductionist version is the "pure" form and the original argument, with words and everything, is a corrupt manifestation of the pure argument. And this, again, is where we see Hellenistic assumptions at work. Incarnation corrupts and makes pure things dirty, or so the thinking goes.

The conclusion should be simple. Truth functions do not represent human language and argumentation accurately at every point. Reduction of human communication to symbols is a shortcut way to analyze communication at a certain level. It is not something that reveals the "real and true" nature of that communication. When the realm of Ps and Qs is ontized, the marvelous subtle-

ties of language are submitted to the authority of a bare-
bones structure—as though a skeleton by itself were better
than a living body.

Abstract Grammar and Vocabulary

Unless we guard ourselves constantly we fall into the trap
of ontizing, and we do it in all sorts of areas. The world
of Forms, or quasi-Forms, is attractive because it is a nice,
comfortable place for the tidy-minded. In this nice place,
very few unpredictable things happen. This has an effect,
not surprisingly, on our understanding of language, even
apart from translation into symbolic notation.

This is the perennial tempation of the grammarian and
lexicographer. Because classical and Christian schools are
in the vanguard of returning to stricter and tighter standards, this will be a perennial temptation for us as well.
And so, coming right to the point, are the rules of grammar
descriptive or prescriptive?

When we teach a foreign language, we tend to teach
it "by the book," that is, in a manner as unlike our acqui-
sition of our native language as possible. With regard to
grammar, we assert that the learning of grammar is the
key to mastery, when actually mastery is the key to grammar. One small example may suffice. I have taken courses
in Latin and I have taught them, and consequently I am
able to inform you that Latin has six tenses. My working knowledge of Latin, however, is very rudimentary
compared to that of English. I have a far better grasp of
English, both with regard to the printed and spoken word.
I am fluent in English and not in Latin. However, I have
no idea how many tenses English has. I am sure I have been
informed at various times, sometimes by my wife, a
longsuffering woman who teaches English, but I keep forgetting. Now how is that lack of knowledge of the number of tenses in my native language no barrier to using
any of them, and using them properly, many times in one

day? How come I know one thing but can't use it well, but I can use another thing with ease but don't know it as well?

Vocabulary provides another important example. When learning another language, the student works out of vocabulary lists and glossaries in the back of the book. How is one to know that *kai* is the Greek word meaning "and, even, also"? That is how it is listed in the vocabulary. But how did a native speaker of Greek come to know what it means? Mastery of a given word comes from having seen it functioning in countless situations, most of which the speaker has entirely forgotten. Someone who looked up a word in the dictionary, who memorized the definitions there, and who could tell you all about the day he learned that word and the circumstances under which he mastered all its definitions would have a wooden mastery indeed.

To overstate my case a little, a man does not have mastery of a word until he is *unable* to tell you how he knows what it means. In other words, someone who is fluent generally has no idea. As an English speaker I have looked up some words in an English dictionary, but that only accounts for a tiny percentage of the words I know. Thorough knowledge of words and grammar and language cannot come from any kind of realist lexical reservation but only from a nominalist world of experience. Every word we use in knowledge has countless little dents in it.

But many, those with the minds of prescriptivist grammarians, view the dictionary as a realm where the meaning of a word resides in a pristine state. They view grammars as a place where the laws governing proper usage come down from a lexical Sinai.

However, this is not stated outright by those guilty of it. If pressed on the question whether grammar is descriptive or prescriptive, they will answer correctly—it has to be descriptive. They sit in Moses' seat, and so we should take heed. But the whole endeavor is treated with such a schoolmarmish severity, because schoolmarms in the front of the classroom must prescribe so as to make us all realize that we had still better obey the rule. I still remember vividly the day I was taught never to begin a sentence with the words *and* or *but*.

But the goal of language instruction should be euphonic precision, not obedience to rules. When obedience to rule governs, the result, as Quintilian so aptly stated, is a piece of work that is equally free of both flaws and virtues.

Of course the prescriptive element legitimately comes in when the language of educated people is described for the student so that the student may be equipped to join the ranks of such people. But nevertheless, when we do not hedge the practice of prescription around with constant warnings and qualifications, prescriptive rules come to be set down as though they existed in their own authority, in their own realm. The rules of grammar have come to be ontized. The meaning of words has come to be ontized. But the world of actual language use is so messy and so complex that only God understands the English language.

This brings us to the relation of logic and reason to the business of human language. The relativist wants to say that there is *no* relation, and the precisionist wants to say there is a precise and settled relation. But neither fit the situation. The logic of words is not the same as the detached, structural, and contentless logic of math or symbolic logic.

Some quirks should help make the problem obvious. Why do "He could not get to sleep, not even with a sedative" and "He could not get to sleep, even with a sedative" mean the same thing? Why does "Don't be surprised if he doesn't get well one of these days" mean that we should not be surprised if he *does* get well? Why do "I couldn't care less" and "I could care less" mean the same thing? Who is in charge of this language? Why do we pronounce the word *one* as though it began with a *wuh*? And what sound does *ough* make? "A rough, dough-faced, thoughtful ploughman strode through the streets of Scarborough; after falling into a slough, he coughed and hiccoughed." This should be read by the learned as "A ruff, doe-faced, thawtful plowman strode throo the streets of Scarboruh; after falling into a sloo, he coffed and hiccupped." Quite a language we have here, and it all has a great deal to do with, I think, William the Conqueror.

The answer to all these questions, and many more, boils down to *just because*. We have "developed" a logical system of signals to enable us to communicate with one another, but the logic of it does not correspond directly to the logic of the mathematical mind. I put "developed" in quotation marks because the capacity to speak is given by God; Adam was created *speaking*. Nevertheless, we do develop specific languages over time, under the providence of God.

The symbols or numbers in a mathematical formula have a denotation, but no connotations to speak of. In addition, the confines of the symbols or numbers we use are very narrow and inflexible. The number 8 means just one thing, for example, and does not on occasion mean more or less than that. Words have both denotations and connotations. Further, words are elastic and can be made to carry additional meanings at any time (or even contradictory meanings). "The water is cold" and "the water is frigid" have the same denotations but not the same connotations.

Thus with mathematical processes the level of certainty is high. However, because of the narrowness and inflexibility of the instruments, the *scope* of certainty is truncated. Add 8 to 8 and you know that you will always get 16. This is quite true, but it does not get one very far. Contrast this with "The eye of the Lord follows all those who fear Him, and underneath are the everlasting arms." For the one who has certain precisionist expectations, this is full of nonsense. How can an incorporeal Spirit have eyes and arms? One person with no soul takes the theological abstractions, necessary in their place, and assumes that this is the whole truth of the matter. Another person with no soul doesn't understand poetry either and assumes that God must have eyes and arms.

Certain conventions of speech can and should be taught. But the teaching is akin to teaching someone what fork should be used as the salad fork; it is *not* like teaching someone the relations between force and mass. Put another way, when we teach proper grammar we are teaching manners, not morals, although (of course) manners are always a moral issue.

Nowhere are these issues better illustrated than with the questions that swirl around the practice of translation. Consider a simple test case, a modification of our earlier sentence about Claudius. Let's generalize him and see what happens. The Latin sentence *Vir feminam amat* can be translated a number of different ways, each with a differing nuance in English. There is no definite article in Latin, and so *vir* can be either *a man* or *the man*. The same goes for *woman*. The verb is in the present tense, which can be rendered three different ways in English. But alas, the word *vir* can also be translated, depending on the context, as *male, husband, honorable man, hero,* or *soldier.* Then of course, because we have no definite article, this is *a male* or *the male, a husband* or *the husband,* and so forth. Not surprisingly, *femina* can also mean *a female* or *the female.* How many different ways do we have of translating this thing? You can do the math. What does it mean? With a precisionist approach, there is no real way of telling. With a rational approach it means that *a man loves a woman,* unless it means something else.

If this looks like relativism, it simply shows how much we have bought into precisionist assumptions. Language is not algebra; words do not have decimal places. And recognition of complexity in an issue *is not relativism.*

What degree of precision is possible in a translation? As always, we should look to Scripture for our model. The Protestant scholastics taught that the Scriptures had a twofold authority, one of substance and the other one verbal. The first was *authoritas rerum*—the authority of the "things" of Scripture, the substance of what was said. This authority pertains to the text of Scripture in the autographs, in the apographs, and also to any "accurate" translations of the apographs. Verbal authority was the *authoritas verborum*, the authority of the words of Scripture, belonging only to the text in the original canonical form, in the original canonical languages.

Now, given this, what *is* an accurate translation? Should it strive for mathematical accuracy? Or is this hopeless? Is there another category, with a different set of "tolerances," which we should call translational accuracy?

We must come to understand incarnational translation, which is to say, understanding translation as interpretation. There are two ways an interpreter can fail. One is through assuming that the languages he works with are like mathematics and that any deviance from that standard should be considered as a failing. This is the way of the man who wants to get the three Latin words *vir feminam amat* into three English words and wants them to be the the same three English words every time. Whenever he works the same math problem he wants to get the same answer. The other fellow fails because he is too loose, rendering those words as *a logging truck hits an elk*.

The *authoritas verborum* is an external and "accidental" authority that falls away in the process of any interpretation, however good. But in considering this we must be careful not to think of a naked, internal essence of a given word, a wordless word, and an outer accidental clothing. It would be better, I think, to speak of the *authoritas rerum* in an incarnational way, with one word "morphing" into another word. This would be in contrast to the idea of taking the "meaning" out of one word, leaving behind its husk, and then transplanting that "meaning" into another word, as though the essential meanings of words were ethereal hermit crabs. We are dealing with people and history, not ideas and abstractions. Of course this is not to deny that we do have an experience of non-articulated "words." I am simply maintaining that the human mind is fundamentally linguistic, and that is a subject for another time.

Consider another angle. The word used in the interpretation has its own authority, its own history. Although not possessing divinely inspired authority, it does have what we might call *linguistic* authority. If the meaning of the interpreted word is put into the new interpreting word, can the guest be unaffected by its new host? And here is another consideration. Do words *age*? What happens once the interpretation has occurred? The words used in the AV of 1611 are not the same now as they were then.

The Greek (Hellenistic!) word for translation or interpretation is *methermeneuo,* from which we get hermeneutics. We know that good translations can be accomplished, because God Himself shows us the pattern: "Behold, a virgin shall be with child, and shall bring forth a son, and they shall call his name *Emmanuel,* which being interpreted is, *God with us*" (Matt. 1:23; cf. Mark 5:41; 15:22; 34; John 1:38, 41; Acts 4:36). In Scripture, translation is *interpretation.* The activities here range from what we would call translation to what we would call interpretive etymology. The rationalistic mind sees this as far too sloppy and wants a master key—and three point landings every time. But they cannot have it; God did not make language the way they dream He did.

My name *Douglas* means *out of the black swamp.* Does it really? Or did it *used* to mean that? *Euangelion* translated means *gospel.* Being interpreted this means *good news,* which is discovered by breaking the compound Greek word in two.

The Old English *cyninga* means *king* the same way that *basileus* means *king*. Or does it?

Ad Verecundium

In any detailed argumentation, appeals to authority come cheap and easy. Nevertheless, in this case they are necessary for two reasons. The first concerns the simple fact that an approach to learning that claims to be grounded in history, and not in the realm of abstractions, cannot afford to be detached from what thinkers and observers throughout history have noted about this problem. For in no way can this be considered a new thing, somehow ushered in by the advent of the silicon chip. However, while the temptation has been present a long time, succumbing to the temptation *as a way of life* is the fruit of modern rationalism. And while we do not wish to blame everything on Descartes, who is, for example, not directly responsible for the Spice Girls, we may certainly mark the ascendancy of Cartesian rationalism as a central part of our difficulty.

The second reason to cite a lot of authorities is perhaps more self-serving. In discussions of this nature, it is very easy for what I would call an "organic approach" to learning to be characterized (sometimes by *both* sides) as nothing more than a sloppy version of the more rationalistic, analytic approach. In other words, there is only one way to study and learn, and that one way can be done badly or well. When this characterization is likely to be made, the best thing the present writer can do, since he really *has* been sloppy on various occasions, is to surround himself with a crowd of worthies. If these eminentoes in the history of thought are saying roughly the same thing he is, then the anticipated *ad hom* can be averted, to the great relief of all.

In certain respects, we are talking about nothing more than keeping the means and ends straight, or maintaining a stable set of priorities. Unfortunately, one of the easiest things in the world a scholar can do is to allow himself to get distracted. Quintilian, the great Roman orator, said of the study of rhetoric, "Therefore, in most instances, we must rely on ourselves, and must study cases with the utmost care, never forgetting that men discovered our art before ever they proceeded to teach it."[1]

Throughout his masterful work, he insists on the general guidance of "rules" to maintain the orator's effectiveness. But at the same time, again and again he warns of the dangers of wooden application. Put another way, eloquence will never be the result of a plug and chug approach.

Dorothy Sayers laments how the language "purists" suceeded in killing the Latin language:

> But if it is dead today, it is because the Classical Scholars killed it by smothering it with too much love. Up to the time of the Revival of Learning, it was a living language, growing and developing like a living language alongside of its children and grandchildren and, like many a hearty and lively grandparent today, picking up much of their speech and slang as it went along.[2]

In other words, with the rise of humanistic and rationalistic scholarship in the Renaissance, a finicky spirit also arose, which said that all forms of messy Latin had to go.

C. S. Lewis makes the same point: "It is largely to the humanists that we owe the curious conception of the 'classical' period in a language, the correct or normative period before which all was immature or archaic and after which all was decadent."[3] He goes on:

> They succeeded in killing the medieval Latin: but not in keeping alive the schoolroom severities of their restored Augustanism. Before they had ceased talking of a rebirth it became evident that they had really built a tomb. Fantastic pains and skill went to its building. Bembo's friend Longolius bound himself with an oath

to abstain not only from every word but from every
number and case of a word that could not be found
in Cicero.[4]

As a result of this rationalistic zeal, a perverse, pursed-
lips standard arose: "A negative conception of excellence
arose: it was better to omit a beauty than to leave in anything that might have the shadow of an offence."[5]

First rationalism and then scientism. Jacques Barzun
put it this way: "When, in the 1890s, the classical curriculum tried to compete with the sciences by becoming 'scientific' too, it signed its own death warrant."[6] What we
call a traditional and classical approach to grammar is often
nothing more than a return to classical education's first
attempts at a compromise with modernity. And if I may
offer a particular complaint here, I have to note that
modern conservative seminaries commonly teach ancient
languages as though they were a form of calculus. The
effect on the life of the church has been profound and
monstrous.

H. L. Mencken observed something similar—

It is never possible for a metaphysician to state his ideas
in plain English. Those ideas, with few exceptions, are
inherently nonsensical, and he is forced to formulate
them in a vague and unintelligible jargon. Of late some
of the stars of the faculty have taken to putting them
into mathematical formulae. They thus become completely incomprehensible to the layman, and gain the
additional merit of being incomprehensible also to
most other metaphysicians.[7]

And in a discussion of teaching, Mencken puts his
finger on a perennial problem with professional modernist
educators:

The aim seems to be to reduce the whole teaching process to a sort of automatic reaction, to discover some
master formula that will not only take the place of com-

petence and resourcefulness in the teacher but that will also create an artificial receptivity in the child. Teaching becomes a thing in itself, separable from and superior to the thing taught. Its mastery is a special business, a sort of transcendental high jumping. A teacher well grounded in it can teach anything to any child, just as a sound dentist can pull any tooth out of any jaw.[8]

As modernists, we have a perverse wish to quantify everything. As educators, we want to be able to quantify every element in the process of education. How else can we prepare the transcript? But while the ability for abstract thinking and quantification are very great gifts of God, they are not *universal* gifts, designed to be applied to everything. They undergird. In the realm of education, the teacher must recognize the existence of countless variables outside his control. And so we end where we began, with the recognition that "rationalism" is not the *telos* of education but rather one useful tool in it, a tool that prepares the student for the real business before him, which is, of course, the cultivation of a love of truth, goodness, and beauty.

As we are engaged in the great work of restoring classical and Christian education, we must be careful. We are leaving behind the swamps of feel-good education, and we do want to restore standards. But there is a strictness that substitutes the aridity of the desert for the muck of the swamp. For our part, we should want neither.

So raise the standard. And lighten up.

Chapter Seven:

A Brief for Greyfriars Hall

Introduction

The idea of formal seminary education dies hard. We have trained so many generations of ministers in this fashion that we can scarcely credit any other way of doing it. We also hear, from time to time, of churches which take pride in having an *uneducated* ministry, and we want nothing to do with that sort of know-nothingism. So we easily slip into the fallacy of thinking that the only alternative to formal, professional seminary training for the ministry is that of informal and unprofessional *lack* of preparation. Because we do not want our pastors to be poorly educated, we routinely ship them off to a seminary. If a young man expresses a desire for the ministry, for all practical purposes, his future plans are set for him. He begins the search to find a seminary that will equip him in finding a pastorate, and then off he goes.

Whenever a false dilemma is presented to us, and this is one of them, we must be careful to avoid being rushed into choosing. Is the only choice really between *no* education on the one hand and *graduate* school education on the other? Of course the ministry should be thoroughly educated, as Dabney effectively argued, but this should not be confused with attending a graduate school.

This essay constitutes a concrete outline for the establishment of a particular kind of ministerial training under the authority of the elders of Community Evangelical Fellowship in Moscow, Idaho. Because it is a particular proposal, specific names, procedures, curricula, etc., will be mentioned and discussed throughout. At the same time, the principles involved are equally applicable in many different church situations. For this reason, the rationale for various proposals will be discussed and defended in greater detail than they perhaps would be in another setting. In this way, the elders of other churches may be able to take advantage of some of the principles addressed here—but with methods more suited to their particular situation.

Some of the positions taken here, either directly or by implication, may strike some as unnecessarily rigid or perhaps even severe. This is not the intention at all. It is freely admitted that various seminaries in the course of their histories have served the cause of Christ ably and well, and that many graduates of seminaries have been among the church's brightest lights. Princeton had a glorious history, for example. But we are not evaluating the system of seminary training on the basis of such individual achievements. We should rather evaluate our system of ministerial training on the basis of the biblical case that can be made for it and on the basis of its tendencies and fruit when considered overall. Princeton did have a glorious history, but where is she now? The evangelical church today is in a miserable and wretched condition, and it must be asserted that our process of seminary education has been one of the central culprits. An unbiblical system, however well-intentioned, will not bear biblical fruit over the course of generations.

The fact remains that, for the most part, seminary education in the United States has become the realm of parachurch organizations (this is generally true of denominational seminaries as well), governed more by the rules of the academy and various secular accrediting agencies than by the rules of the Church, which someone once said was the pillar and ground of the truth. No one disputes that parachurch organizations have done good and, in some instances, have done much good. But Christ is the head of the *Church*, and He did not leave the evangelization and discipleship of the world to freewheeling parachurch ministries. The fact that good has been done is a testimony to the goodness and mercy of God. But it is not a basis for us to continue with a system of ministerial education for the Church that is not conducted within the Church or effectively overseen by the Church.

A system of ordination has developed where seminaries provide the rigorous "graduate school" education, while the local churches are supposed to determine a candidate's fitness for ministry. The elders of a local church, for their part, assume that if a student made it through an approved seminary, he must be a fit candidate. The result is that many have found their way into ministry because they have shown a great aptitude for graduate level study and test-taking. The point here is not whose fault this is but rather to show just one of many ways in which the system we have adopted has set us up for a fall. Human nature being what it is, we may continue to expect much more of the same kind of thing if we continue on the same course. The disease has so far progressed that we now tend to assume that graduate school honors are the qualifications we should look for in a ministerial candidate. Paul's requirements for a godly ministry are set aside, and we think that it is all right to do this because the man whose marriage and family are a stretcher case (and got that way while he was working his guts out in seminary) nevertheless *has professional certification*. He has the right papers on the wall, embossed and signed. This is nothing less than the capitulation of the evangelical church to the bureaucratic mind. Nothing good can come of it, and the sooner we find the way of repentance the better.

The pastoral epistles have that name for a reason. Be-

cause Christians are accustomed to treating the entire Bible
as a book of inspirational quotes, we sometimes miss specific instructions that are addressed to particular officers. The Bible is the covenant document of the Church,
and many of the requirements do not have direct application to individuals.

For example, in the famous passage about the inspiration of the Word of God, Paul says that the Bible builds
up the "man of God" so that he may be complete,
"equipped for every good work" (2 Tim. 3:17). This is not
addressed to every Christian (although it may be extended
to them by analogy). It is addressed to *the man of God*,
the minister—one who is responsible before the Lord for
the spiritual well-being of others. This one needs to be
able to rebuke, admonish, exhort, etc.

In 2 Timothy, Paul also teaches us how the leadership
of the church is to reproduce itself. He says:

> You therefore, my son, be strong in the grace that is
> in Christ Jesus. And the things that you have heard
> from me among many witnesses, commit these to
> faithful men who will be able to teach others also.
> (2 Tim. 2:1–2)

This is not a requirement that every Christian should
disciple others in such a way that they are able in turn to
disciple others. When this does happen in an informal way,
we are all grateful for it. The Bible encourages this sort
of instruction—for example, the older women are told to
teach and instruct the younger women (Titus 2:3–5). This
does not mean that the older women are officers in the
Church. Rather it means that a general pattern of teaching and encouragement is to pervade the Church, with the
more mature leading and instructing the less mature. This
happens naturally in the home and in any community. But
this informal work explains only a part of the apostolic
instruction to the church.

The charge to Timothy *here* refers to the duty of church leadership to reproduce itself. What Timothy had heard from the apostle Paul he was to pass on to faithful men. These faithful men in turn were to teach and instruct others. This clearly occurs within the context of the work of the church. This is how Paul trained Timothy in evangelistic and pastoral work, and he here tells Timothy to go and do the same.

Similarly, the Great Commission was given to the apostles, but in a way that ensures the commission is self-perpetuating. Christ told the apostles to teach obedience to *everything* that Christ had commanded (Matt. 28:18–20). This would of course include His last command, that the nations be discipled. This means that the apostles who received the initial commission were to pass it on to the next generation and the next generation was to do the same. But this commission is given to the *Church*—not to every individual Christian. This means that the leadership of the Church is to receive the commission, and the leadership of the Church is to pass on the commission.

Our generation is so individualistic that we tend to interpret everything in private terms. The notion that God may have given the government of the church a set of instructions for the preparation and training of future leaders, their qualifications, their duties, etc., is entirely foreign to us. But this is one foreign notion we must learn to make our own; we must come to speak the language of Scripture again.

As we return to a more biblical pattern of training future elders and ministers, we do not expect a transformation overnight. The current system has a tremendous amount of inertia behind it. As we present an alternative to seminary education, we do not expect seminaries or seminarians to go away—and we are very happy to cooperate with those seminaries that remain faithful to the Word of God. In presenting what we believe to be a more biblical approach, we do not want to inculcate a perfectionistic attitude that demands everything be reformed immediately. This only ensures that nothing substantive will ever change.

Nevertheless, a local church that takes its mission of evangelism and discipleship seriously should be able to fully train leaders for service in the local church. *Any calling that is incapable of reproducing itself is incompetent in that calling.*

This training is for her own leaders in the years to come. A thriving church can easily assume that it "has it covered" because its current elders are doing a fine job and its current pastor preaches well and looks healthy. Everyone has trouble imagining what the church will look like in fifty years when none of the current leaders is alive. No one even thinks about it. But Charles de Gaulle put it well when he said that the graveyards are full of indispensable men. That day will come whether we want it to or not. A church that does not think of establishing continuity with the future generations of that same church is, in principle, a church populated by short term and anti-covenantal thinkers.

When a pastor retires or dies, the usual tendency is to scramble, form a pastoral search committee, and . . . you know the rest of the drill. An outsider, someone who is not in touch with the local and organic life of that particular congregation, is called, and he steps into the pastorate. His paper qualifications were impressive, and his pulpit delivery while he was "candidating" was good, but the fact remains that churches that get a pastor this way are basically getting a mail-order bride.

What about calling and costs? Because the training being undertaken is within the context of the church *for the benefit of the church*, the costs for this education should be borne by the church. This would be a major first step in removing from our churches the mentality of the hireling professional.

Obviously, when something is offered for "free," it might encourage some who do not have a genuine call from the Lord to take advantage of the opportunity to study. But as men aspire to the ministry, they should not do so in an autonomous fashion, as though they were the sole arbiter of whether this is their calling or not. Studying for the ministry is *not* like studying dentistry or architecture. With other such callings, a person who has the intelligence, money, and willingness to work can make it happen. A person who is spending his own money is really a consumer—a customer. He is purchasing goods or services. In the case of seminary, he is purchasing graduate-level theological instruction. This means he has authority over what he has purchased.

The call to the ministry and preparation for it should not be approached the same way. Of course the individual should understand himself to be called, but this by itself is not sufficient. The church, which will be the beneficiary of the training, should be involved in the decision to train someone for the ministry. Men should not be preparing for the ministry unless there is good reason to believe that they have the gifts and calling for that ministry. This understanding should be shared by others in the church, particularly by the leaders of the church. Far too many pious young men, zealous for ministry, have been misled into thinking that intense desire for ministry is an adequate substitute for ability and call.

The church that provides the training should testify that she believes a young man is called to the work of ministry by paying for the costs of his instruction. If a church has sent someone to be trained at another church, then that sending church can add her testimony by paying for books or helping with living expenses. Obviously this will not be done unless the churches in question have a good understanding of the student's character and ability.

It is a truism that if you don't name it, someone else will. The intentions can be great and the plans well laid, but if nothing is done, then people are going to call what you are doing a seminary. This makes it necessary to be somewhat aggressive in calling it something else and to insist upon calling it that—perhaps to the point of being thought belligerent.

I propose that in our situation we call this course of training *Greyfriars Hall,* and it is a ministerial hall, not a seminary. The Greyfriars church in Scotland was the place where the Solemn League and Covenant was first subscribed, and it is a name that is important to everyone who loves the work of reformation. Graduates of this hall would *not* receive a professional degree or anything that sounded like a professional degree. The bureaucratic system that governs the granting of all such degrees is well-entrenched, and any attempt to compete with them while using their terminology is not likely to be blessed. A ministerial hall avoids the assumptions that govern the running of graduate schools. As a hall for study, there is no pretense of "professionalism."

At the same time, the phrase *ministerial hall* does indicate a rigorous preparation for the ministry. An informal, casual, and undefined system of education simply will not do. If an apprentice for the ministry were simply to hang around the leadership of a church for several years, he would no doubt learn many valuable things, but mostly he would simply learn "how things are done around here."

The prospective minister who graduates from this hall will receive a letter of commendation stating that he has performed his work ably and well, and that the instructors and elders overseeing the training of this man have learned enough about him to be able to say he is qualified for the Christian ministry, in his character, history, and gifts.

Anyone interested in obtaining a copy of the curriculum of Greyfriars Hall may contact us.

Chapter Eight:

Why Evangelical Colleges Aren't

Two separate educational movements exist within the evangelical world, one old and one new, and they are clearly on a collision course.

One thing sure does lead to another, and he who says A must say B. The widespread parental challenge to the tax-financed secularism of the government school system is by now common knowledge. By the thousands, parents are saying, "Not with my kid, you don't," and have enrolled their children in private academies, have started to homeschool, have taken advantage of tutorial services, and so forth. However, this growing challenge to secular education has some necessary ramifications in the years to come, for which established evangelical *colleges* are singularly unprepared. The reasons for this are legion, but all reduce to the embarrassing fact that there is far too much jelly in *evangelical*.

Parents are not about to spend years sacrificing themselves to provide a private Christian education only to give it all away when an "evangelical" college offers to undo all they accomplished in the previous twelve years. A graduate of an evangelical establishment like Wheaton has a far better chance of receiving a diploma in trendy leftism than his counterpart down the road at Leviathan State U. Colleges like Westmont, Gordon, and Bethel all have a fine reputation to uphold; unfortunately, upholding it in this day and age can mean schmoozing it up with the spirit of the age. And even when nothing overtly objectionable is done as a result, the college has to remain bland enough not to cross accrediting agencies with anything like a distinctively Christian view of the world. Brer Evangelical, he lay low.

But studied neutrality is impossible, and obnoxious examples are cropping up more and more frequently, in fulfillment of a collegial application of the dictum that a man who doesn't stand for something will fall for anything. We now find the *Zeitgeist* appearing in raunchy requirements for classes, "revivals" that resemble group therapy confessionals, and urbane professorial "muddling-about" with postmodern relativism. And then top it all off with the fact that Wheaton even *has* an Office of Minority Affairs.

At Leviathan U, the Christian students are wary and know that the faculty are largely in the employ of old slewfoot. But at Wheaton, the Billy Graham Center is right across the street, the jargon is full of all the right God-words, and revivals that don't change a damn thing still manage to appear with some regularity.

But parents who have spent the earlier years educating themselves on educational issues are not going to forget what they have learned simply because their children are now in thirteenth grade. Nor will they look the other way just because the charade is appropriately baptized. Such parents will beware of wolves in sheepskins, and this leads us to consider why many of them will come to the conclusion that evangelical colleges . . . aren't.

For the most part, these colleges were established before the cultural fruit of the antithesis between secularism and Christianity was quite as apparent as it is now. These colleges were founded over a century ago, and the Christian school movement has only developed within the last twenty years. The Christian school movement was formed in self-conscious reaction to the regnant foolishness, while the Christian colleges, proudly part of the establishment, are a significant part of that foolishness. These two movements are already looking at one another across a great divide.

According to a popular mythology in more conservative circles, the nineteenth century was a time of strong traditional values, when it was actually a monkey house of radicalism. The traditional values, such as they were, were the harvest of what had been planted in previous centuries—vestiges of Christendom. But the crop that was being *sown* in that era is the one we are harvesting now. The fact that this was occurring was apparent at that time to foresighted individuals, but there were not many of them. Apostate utopias were still at the blueprint stage, or to change the metaphor drastically, the pudding that proves had not yet been eaten.

In the nineteenth century, when most of these evangelical colleges were being established, they were themselves a leading manifestation of this democratizing spirit, this utopian pragmatism. Our nation was young, full of beans and democratic zeal, and American evangelicals were industrious in making the democratization of religion one of their central distinctives. Among many other things, this was reflected in the colleges they built. The principles institutionalized in the evangelical colleges at that time have now borne the fruit, fruit which contemporary evangelical parents are refusing to eat.

A great deal of energy could be preserved if in our reforms we would spend more time trying to identify the genuine point of departure. In the '60s, prayer was banished from the government school system, and the Beatles came to America. Traditional conservatives proved themselves masters of the *post hoc* fallacy and have spent a considerable amount of time, money, and energy trying to get back to the way we were before all that. But the roots of our disorder go much deeper, and without getting into the details, we have to identify it with the American abandonment of the idea of Christendom. This abandonment did not come all at once, but by the time of the establishment of most denominational and interdenominational evangelical colleges, the divorce had been finalized.

We like to think of the Church as victim, but on our continent, the Church has largely played the role of instigator. The good intentions involved did nothing more than make the church a blind instigator. Like it or not, the church necessarily has a position of leadership. The declension of culture in America is comparable to well-meaning but naive parents who raise a child without discipline and without instilling self-control and who are then shocked at the *extent* of the rebellion apparent when that child gets away from home. The extent of our current rebellion can be seen in our cultural parade of sodomites, cotqueans, health nazis, and feminists. But the *nature* of this rebellion was established long before. There were women in pulpits and standing at altars long before they were seated in the cockpits of F-16s.

Cultures come to resemble their gods—"They that make them are like unto them; so is every one that trusteth in them" (Ps. 115:8 KJV; cf. v. 4). The new society, following evangelicalism, emphasized personal individual choice. This meant that the confessional approach to higher education had to be abandoned, and the elective system was brought in to replace it. Churches were disestablished and began to compete for customers, just like Sears & Roebuck. Saint Paul used to travel around the ancient Roman world, preaching the word and seeking disciples. Our churches began to hustle around the block, looking for clients and customers. Religious colleges were operating in the same strange world and began to compete for students with even *less* of a confessional interest than the churches now had. For everyone was now in pursuit of customers, and as the world of business teaches us, the customer is always right.

The market system works just fine when we are seeking the kind of toothpaste that suits us best. But when the true, the good, and the beautiful are made into elective courses, no one should be surprised when freshmen consistently sign up for the far more popular courses promoting the false, the wrong, and the ugly. When colleges ceased passing on an inherited body of knowledge and began catering to the interests and desires of the public, the destruction was complete. The fact that many of the colleges which ceased passing on the tradition were called "evangelical" mattered not in the slightest.

But the appearance of market freedom is just that, an appearance. Elitism is inescapable; the dominance of egalitarianism simply means that the established elite must deck themselves out in the name of supposedly neutral standards. Evangelical colleges have agreed to burn their incense to the emperor and now regularly come before secular accrediting agencies and boards, hat in hand. "Please, sir, may we please teach some scratch-'n'-sniff form of the Christian faith?" Well, all right . . . for now.

This hunger for approval in disreputable places has had a predictable effect: "How can ye believe, which receive honour one of another, and seek not the honour that cometh from God only?" (John 5:44 KJV). The pecking order has been established, and those institutions that hunger for academic respectability must respect the pecking order. This means that colleges that want accreditation must get their faculty from previously-approved institutions and must vow never to do anything that seriously challenges the existing order. They must determine to be the very model of kennel-fed Christianity.

Complaints about the bizarre fruit of all this are common because they are too easy. Postmodern whimwham presents an easy target. But we have spent several centuries getting here, and a stern letter to the denominational magazine will really accomplish nothing. Our only real hope is that the parents currently showing such zeal in the sound education of their younger children will not be too tired, when the time comes, to turn their attention to the establishment of small but genuine colleges.

Chapter Nine:

Classical Learning and the Christian College

Introduction

Since the government schools are collapsing, many Christian parents have taken the cue and have enrolled their children in a local, private Christian school. Many others have begun to homeschool. Over the last twenty-five years, our country has seen a dramatic educational revolution in this heartening establishment of homeschools and private Christian academies. This turn of events is a direct response to the visible bankruptcy of the modern education establishment. The point of this essay is not to rehearse the failures of our government primary and secondary schools; that has been thoroughly established elsewhere.[1]

Many of these rescued children, kept safely out of the mainstream, have been *educated*. Coming to the point of graduation, the students from these schools and homeschools have formed a vanguard of well-educated Christian students who have begun to think about . . . college. And because they have received a Christian education up to this point, it only makes sense for them to consider the various Christian colleges throughout the country. But as they and their parents examine the literature from these colleges, and as they talk with students who attend them, what they find out is frequently unsettling.[2] Some of the underlying reasons for this discontent will be explored in this essay.

Modern evangelical colleges were established, for the most part, in the last century. They were founded before the bankruptcy of relativistic humanism was making the front page every night. Consequently, most of these colleges do not have a clear sense of the antithesis between Christianity and all other contending faiths. This is particularly true with regard to those other worldview faiths that pretend not to be faiths—those that masquerade as objective "science" or "reason" or as "the results of modern scholarship." In fact, so many appeals are made to "most scholars" that the young student may be tempted to try to find articles at the library listed under *Most Scholars' Review*. Even those Christian colleges that have managed to retain some doctrinal integrity with regard to their Christian commitments have capitulated to the spirit of academic "neutrality." The only place where Christianity is still practically confessed is by (perhaps) the chaplain and a few theology profs who are scattered around a handful of spiritual reservations across campus. But in the classroom, where the business of the college is done—in economics, history, philosophy— confessional, applied Christianity is entirely absent. In short, most Christian colleges are arguably part of the *secular,* higher-education establishment.

Christian colleges have not presented the biblical antithesis between the Christian faith on the one hand and the general helplessness and decline seen pervading our culture on the other. Consequently, such Christian colleges are condemned to share in that broader cultural decline—in morality, in academic rigor, and in discipline. Oftentimes, the motto of the Christian college appears to be, "Anything the world can do, we can do five years later." In some cases, Christian colleges can be seen clambering on to a bandwagon just when the secularists have tired of it and are getting off.

A Christian college is not a college where many people

would go to heaven if the entire campus were destroyed by a giant meteor. A Christian college is a place where a college education is imparted in a biblical, covenant-keeping fashion. Christian colleges have departed from this high calling and important mission because they were distracted into thinking they were perpetually consigned to be a little sister to the big, secular, "grown-up" universities: "You know, where we get all our Ph.D.s." Because of this tendency to mimic and follow after, we must address both the ills of Christian colleges today as well as the sandy foundations of secular universities together. And as Dylan put it, you don't have to be a weatherman to tell which way the wind is blowing.

So relativism, in the realm of higher, secular education, has come to the end of its tether. And like a stupid but persistent dog, still alive but discouraged, the relativists keep yanking, trying to get free of the constraints imposed on them through God's created order. Our secular college and university system has a death wish. This is not surprising; in Scripture we see the autonomous death wish. Wisdom states, "But he who sins against me wrongs his own soul; all those who hate me *love death*" (Prov. 8:36). Apart from God and His Christ, the world around us is an unconnected series of multiversities. This is why multicultural diversity is so popular on the campus these days. When one has no nails, one acts as though the pieces of wood are *supposed* to be apart like they are. Men and women without Christ must suppose that they live not in a universe but in a multiverse. In the truest sense of the term, it is a blank verse. A *universe* can only be spoken of coherently by Christians. The *university* is a Christian concept and grew out of a Christian worldview. In Christ everything coheres. Apart from Him, nothing does. The apostle Paul put it this way:

> And He is before all things, and *in Him all things consist*. He is the head of the body, the church, who is the

beginning, the firstborn from the dead, *that in all things He may have the preeminence.* For it pleased the Father that in Him all the fullness should dwell, and by Him to reconcile all things to Himself, by Him, whether things on earth or things in heaven, having made peace through the blood of His cross. (Col. 1:17–20)

Everything must be brought into submission to Christ. He is the Lord, the only One to whom intellectual and academic allegiance may be given. Again, Paul:

For though we walk in the flesh, we do not war according to the flesh. For the weapons of our warfare are not carnal but mighty in God for pulling down strongholds, casting down arguments and every high thing that exalts itself against the knowledge of God, bringing *every thought into captivity* to the obedience of Christ. . . . (2 Cor. 10:3–5)

A godless, Christless cosmos—impossible even to imagine, even for the sake of argument—is a fragmented pile. Worse than a pile, it is j^&%n*&i^%—fully and completely senseless. Even such random keystrokes exhibit far more order than is conceivable without Him; they move in a straight line, left to right. Order and sense are inescapable because we live in the world God made. Education instructs a student how to think about the world, how to think about the universe. But he cannot be taught how to think about the universe *if he doesn't know he lives in one.*

J. Gresham Machen, who was classically educated, applied this truth with characteristic brilliance. He said,

The Christian cannot be satisfied so long as any human activity is either opposed to Christianity or out of all connection with Christianity. Christianity must pervade not merely all nations, but also all of human thought. The Christian, therefore, cannot be indifferent to any branch of earnest human endeavor. It must all be brought into some relation to the gospel. It must be studied either in order to be demonstrated as false, or else in order to be made useful in advancing the Kingdom of God. The Church must seek to conquer not merely every man for Christ, but also the whole of man. We are accustomed to encourage ourselves in our discouragements by the thought of the time when every knee shall bow and every tongue confess that Jesus is Lord. No less inspiring is the other aspect of the great consummation. That will also be a time when doubts have disappeared, when every contradiction has been removed, when all of science converges to one great conviction, when all of art is devoted to one great end, when all of human thinking is permeated by the refining, ennobling influence of Jesus, when every thought has been brought into subjection to the obedience of Christ.[3]

In considering the idea of a Christian college, it should be obvious that no solution can be found through providing an ecclesiastical whitewash for relativism. No alternative can be found by aping it either. The early church was privileged to watch classical, educated paganism collapse in its epistemological exhaustion. We have a similar opportunity, but we are currently squandering it. The ancients pagans had no *arche*—no point of coherence for all things. The problem of the One and the Many was beyond the capacity of their autonomous philosophy. Their great thinkers could see all things as One, but they then could not account for plurality. Or they could assume that all was Flux—but then nothing tied together. They had no foundation for thinking that the universe could be *one* place, in which particular, *distinct* things happened. The same dilemma afflicts modern secularists and pagans. And as Charles Cochrane points out, the early church responded with a *true* alternative, a bedrock trust in the Triune God of Scripture:

As against these notions, it asserted that the true start-ing-point for thought and action must remain for ever invisible to the eye of the flesh. This was to alter the entire perspective and to maintain that, for all men without exception, the question of primary importance was not so much their capacity for thinking as the pre-suppositions which governed their thought. And, from this standpoint, faith in the God of revelation was proposed as indispensable to full understanding.[4]

Abandoning the arm of the flesh, believers echoed Ambrose who affirmed *credo ut intelligam*—I believe in order that I might understand. This honest word was, as Proverbs says, like a kiss on the lips. Again, Cochrane:

Thus envisaged, however, the Deity presented itself, not as an object of, but as the basis for, experience, the God "in whom we live and move and are." . . . By the Christians, the radical defect in classical accounts of genesis was ascribed to the inadequacy of the start-ing-point furnished by the "scientific" imagination. On the other hand, they themselves professed to discover in the God of revelation a principle by virtue of which it became possible to construct an adequate picture of nature or the physical world. In the light of that principle, the cosmos presented itself as a world of real, concrete, individual substances, each and every one of which found a "natural" expression in orderly but unimpeded development leading to its appropriate end. Thus conceived, however, the world of nature was neither self-generating nor self-fulfilling, but depended absolutely upon the intelligent and beneficent support of God as its creator and preserver.[5]

Modern paganism is in the same shape her older sister was in just before she collapsed. The difference is that modern Christian academic onlookers interpret the writh-ing of her death throes as a sign of vigor, health, and a bright tomorrow. "I'll have what *she's* having." But not-withstanding the foolishness of the Church, modern paganism remains filled with despair. Where does education *begin*? What is the starting point—what is the frame of reference? There are really only two choices in life, and consequently only two choices in *education for life*. We may choose between the living God and Whirl. Carl Becker observes:

> If we wished to reduce eight centuries of intellectual history to an epigram, we could not do better than to borrow the words of Aristophanes, "Whirl is king, having deposed Zeus." Perhaps the most important consequence of this revolution is that we look about in vain for a semblance of the old authority, the old absolute, for any stable foothold from which to get a running start. Zeus, having been deposed, can no longer serve as a first premise of thought. It is true we may still believe in Zeus; many people do. Even scientists, historians, philosophers still accord him the customary worship. But this is no more than a personal privilege, to be exercised in private, as formerly, in Protestant countries, Papists were sometimes permitted to celebrate mass in private chapels. No serious scholar would now postulate the existence and goodness of God as a point of departure for explaining the quantum theory or the French revolution. If I should venture, as certain historians once did, to expound the thought of the eighteenth century as having been foreordained by God for the punishment of a perverse and stiff-necked generation, you would shift uneasily in your chairs, you would "register" embarrassment, and even blush a little to think that a trusted colleague should exhibit such bad taste. The fact is that we have no first premise. Since Whirl is king, we must start with the whirl, the mess of things as presented in experience.[6]

But educators who start with Whirl must also end with Whirl—those who are anti-Christ soon discover they are also anti-knowledge. In other words, the starting point of knowledge *must be the fear of the Lord*. If this is true of knowledge, it is equally true of the pursuit of knowledge. And colleges are institutions dedicated to the organized and institutional pursuit of knowledge. But this means that the starting point for all colleges and universities must also be the fear of the Lord. The only sound epistemology for scholarship in *any* discipline is found in faith and obedience: "The fear of the Lord is the beginning of knowledge, but fools despise wisdom and instruction" (Prov. 1:7). As Cochrane points out in a footnote, this preeminence of Christ over all of life is clearly a New Testament doctrine (Col. 1:17). If this is true, then why would campus life be excluded?

As Cornelius Van Til observed, moderns think they understand themselves. As Becker's writing evidences, even in their despair, they think that despair makes sense. But a man cannot even say, "Everything is senseless," without making sense; rebellious man is trapped in the world *God* made and not the world he can only partially and inconsistently imagine—

> Modern man thinks he understands himself. This is the grand delusion of the day. Goethe expressed the nature of this delusion well when he said that when the individual speaks it is, alas, no longer the individual that speaks. The principle of individuation involved in modern man and, for the matter of that, in ancient philosophy, is that of pure chance. It is the night in which all cows are black or blackness. The principle of speech, of universality, of unity, of light involved in modern philosophy, and for the matter of that in ancient philosophy, is that of abstract rationality. It is the day in which all cows are white or whiteness.[7]

As Christians, we are hobbled in our obedience to the teaching of Scripture through our disobedient reversal of God's teaching. Turning the insight of Ambrose on its head, we have come to think that we must understand in order to believe. This means, we think, that an *unbelieving* understanding is the beginning of the fear of the Lord. Just to say this out loud is enough of a refutation for any believing heart. But the structure of the curricula at countless Christian colleges reflects just this misunderstanding. The idea is that there are neutral zones in which truth may be pursued, whether or not the scholar in pursuit loves God. Such thinking strikes at the heart of what it means to have a Christian worldview. And the development of a biblical worldview should be at the heart of a Christian college's mission.

A good example of this mentality, popular among Christian academics, can be found in the book *Science Held Hostage* by Howard Van Till, Davis Young, and Clarence Menninga. According to the subtitle, the book sets out to provide a critique of both creation science and evolutionism. In reality the book is a testimony of epistemological confusion and sin. Part II of this book aims to offer a critique of creation science. The central point made in this section is that "a commitment to the 'scientific creationist' picture of cosmic history has functioned to diminish the demand for both craft competence and professional integrity." One moon dust example cited was considered as "intolerable violations of the standards of professional integrity that should characterize the work of natural scientists." Throughout this section of the book, the central attack on the creation scientists is on their *competence* and *integrity*.

When they turn to the devotees of naturalistic scientism in Part III, the treatment alters considerably. This section is radically different from their treatment of the creationists. Many of the criticisms are on the mark, but they are applied with kid gloves. Carl Sagan, for example, was lauded for producing a "Cosmos . . . [which was] well grounded in the results of scientific investigation." Sagan, furthermore, deserves "considerable credit." Not only that, he exhibited "an admirable concern" for preserving our natural resources. In short, he is not at all like that nincompoop Henry Morris.

The reason for making this point is to illustrate what, for these authors, is the *real* "tie that binds." Their Christian brothers are admonished with a meat axe for failing to meet the epistemologically confused standards of scientific academia while God-hating atheistic academics are commended, praised, and engaged in mild argument. Throughout the book the bonds of collegiality are visibly much stronger than the bonds of Christian fellowship, and it is clear they would fear excommunication from academic respectability far more than they would fear excommunication from any believing covenant community. The ultimate sneer for them is to say that a man is not "a natural scientist." To be sure, mild admonishment may be applied to the fellow down the hall who hates and rejects God, but what is that kind of trifle among colleagues?

This is not to say that the creation scientists should be immune from criticism from fellow Christians. If they deserve it, and they frequently do, then it must be offered. The work of the creation scientists has truly been a mixed bag; some are genuinely helpful, and some, like the attempts to institute the teaching of a "neutral" creationism in the government schools, have been a thoroughgoing embarrassment. But criticism should not be offered by any Christian who has previously sold his birthright for a beaker full of pottage—such as Drs. Van Till, Young, and Menninga.

The source of the problem is obvious in Part I. The authors utterly fail to recognize the impossibility of epistemic neutrality in scientific endeavors. They put their aspiration this way: "Provided that they do their scientific work in conformity with the accepted standards for competence and integrity and in the context of the community of professional natural scientists, persons with vastly differing religious commitments can and do work together toward the common goal of understanding the behavior of the physical universe—the object of scientific investigation." In another place, they say,

> Science held hostage by any ideology or belief system, whether naturalistic or theistic, can no longer function effectively to gain knowledge of the physical universe. When the epistemic goal of gaining knowledge is replaced by the dogmatic goal of providing warrant for one's personal belief system or for some sectarian creed, the superficial activity that remains may no longer be called natural science.

In other words, any Christian who seeks, while in the laboratory, to remember any truth he learned anywhere else is "holding science hostage." According to these authors, science must be autonomous: "'No truth from outside these four walls' is *our* motto!" This is excepting, of course, the truth of militant scientific agnosticism espoused by these authors—for *that* must be imported to the lab just as surely as stories about Noah and the ark. If, for example, radical greens impose their environmentalist dogma on some scientific study of the environment, the problem is not that they are imposing dogma on natural science. Rather, the difficulty is that they are imposing *false* dogma on natural science. The same goes for fundamentalist Christians, who are fully capable of imposing their false understanding of Scripture on scientific studies.

By distorting sphere sovereignty, these authors have embraced intellectual schizophrenia. What one believes to be true in one location (church), one must forget when entering the other church he attends (the lab). At the risk of sounding revolutionary, if something is false we should reject it, regardless of the source. And if it is true, we must remember and cherish it, never mind where we go. For these authors to insist that Christians should forget certain truths when they come into the laboratory and pick them up again at the door when they go home is as irrational as to argue that Christians should only hold to the doctrine of the Incarnation every second Tuesday. Why not the other way around? Why not teach evolution in church and look for creation in the lab? Why don't we all just forget the whole thing, grab a beer, and watch the game?

The effect of the teaching of these authors is to trivialize and marginalize the truths of the Christian faith. That being the case, they should simply admit what they are up to, leave Calvin College, and go to a college that is openly evolutionary—Wheaton, say. In short, on Christian college campuses, this repudiation of Christian knowledge is, in the final analysis, a repudiation of *any* knowledge. The relativistic colleges and universities have come to this realization—this is what lies behind deconstruction's denial of objective meaning in a text. On the secular campus, truth is what works "for you." This epistemological cancer is not as advanced on Christian campuses, but it is pervasive, and without biblical treatment it is terminal. The time is coming when the Christianity of the current evangelical colleges will be a dim and hazy memory—just as it is with Harvard today. "Did you know that Wheaton used to be a Christian school?" *Really?*

The foregoing demonstrates the necessity for Christian colleges to maintain a *Christian worldview*. Now the use of popular words like "worldview" is always dangerous. As words enter into common currency, they can soon cease to be helpful as they become "buzzwords"—words that evoke a certain response but still remain nebulous and undefined. *Worldview* is in danger of becoming just such a word; it is certainly used frequently, but we must really have a clear idea of what we mean by it. Earlier we referred to Paul's teaching that every thought is to be made captive to Christ—

> For though we walk in the flesh, we do not war according to the flesh. For the weapons of our warfare are

not carnal but mighty in God for pulling down strongholds, casting down arguments and every high thing
that exalts itself against the knowledge of God, bringing every thought into captivity to the obedience of
Christ, and being ready to punish all disobedience when
your obedience is fulfilled." (2 Cor. 10:3–6)

As we apply this text, we may consequently define
a *Christian worldview as the framework of assumptions about
reality, all of which are in submission to Christ.* A Christian worldview is not defined as a worldview held by someone who is a Christian. Christians can do "non-Christian"
actions, and in the same way, Christians can certainly *think*
"non-Christian" thoughts. Now, we are not saved by our
righteous thinking anymore than we are saved by our righteous actions. We may see sin in ourselves or others without concluding that the "sinner" doesn't know God at all.
At the same time, this does not alter the duty we have,
with regard to our sanctification, *to think as Christians.*
The basic framework of Christian worldview assumptions
is discussed briefly below.

Students trained in a Christian worldview will certainly know the gospel. Knowing the gospel consists of
two basic parts: knowing the condition of man and knowing the provision of God in Christ. The condition of man
is that he is dead in his sins (Eph. 2:1–2), and the provision of God in Christ is that the God/man died on the
cross for His people (Eph. 5:25) and was raised to life for
their justification (Rom. 4:25)—and all in accordance with
the Scripture (1 Cor. 15:1–4).

The gospel brings individuals into a covenant relationship with God. This does not mean their knowledge
of God is instantly complete or has been perfected; it
means their knowledge of God is genuine and real. A
Christian's process of sanctification includes growing in
the knowledge of the majesty and glory of God. This
growth means that a Christian worldview is maturing as

well. There are three important aspects of this. First is the Creator/creature distinction. This is critical: God's thoughts are not like ours (Is. 55:7–9). Our thinking is *utterly* dependent upon Him. God is not "one of us." Second is the holiness and goodness of God—we must grow in knowledge of His goodness (Ex. 34:6), and we must come to know our own hearts apart from Christ (Rom. 8:12–13; 1 Pet. 2:11). Third, the student must come to acknowledge the sovereignty of God—there is not one square inch of creation that can claim independence from God. God's sovereign authority extends to everything (Amos 3:6; Rom. 11:36; and countless other passages).

This will result in knowledge of the *antithesis*—the same antithesis Christian colleges have lost. Because God is sovereign over all things, everything is related to Him in some way. Because the Bible tells us that sin is real, everything is either in submission to God or in rebellion against Him. Every person is either in submission or in rebellion. Every action is either in submission or in rebellion. Every thought is either in submission or in rebellion (Col. 2:6–10). *No neutrality exists anywhere.*

The modern opium dream that education can be religiously neutral should be, in our minds, equivalent to the question of whether or not, to use Dabney's phrase, "schoolrooms should be located under water or in dark caverns." Neutrality about the ultimate questions can be *pretended* in education, but it cannot be accomplished. Therefore, all schools—and all departments—must confess that Jesus Christ is Lord over all. Again, consider Dabney:

> Every line of true knowledge must find its completeness as it converges on God, just as every beam of daylight leads the eye to the sun. If religion is excluded from our study, every process of thought will be arrested before it reaches its proper goal. The structure of thought must remain a truncated cone, with its proper apex lacking.[8]

Because a Christian college is Christian, the fear of the Lord must be at the heart of the curriculum. But there is another aspect to this discussion that applies to all Christian liberal arts colleges. This is the importance of *classical* education—an education grounded in the culture of the West. To resort to a commonplace, when parents teach their children to speak, the language they teach is the language they themselves speak. In other words, the young are always educated by *their* elders. God has placed them in *this* particular cultural river; our children have no ability to flow in a different stream. This principle is recognized clearly when we are talking about parents and their children—just one generation. But it applies, just as clearly, when we take our grandparents and ancestors into account—all the way back to the birth of our Lord in the reign of Caesar Augustus, and before that to the covenant made with Abraham, and before that to the fall of our father Adam. *Education cannot be successfully detached from our cultural river and turned into a small private pond.* If any such attempt is made, the result will be a *poor* cultural education, not a culturally neutral education.

This is not being said in a xenophobic way or from any desire to react mindlessly away from the modern trendiness of multiculturalism. If this duty of cultural education is neglected, the result will *not* be appreciation for other cultures but a poor training in our own. The rising generation of new Christian colleges must therefore encourage each other in the pursuit of cultural excellence.

This means an education that is thoroughly and unabashedly Christian. Theology is the point of integration for all the sciences and it is the study of what the Triune God has revealed in Scripture. It must be strongly emphasized that classical and Christian colleges must therefore be *evangelical historic Protestant* colleges, rejecting both the mind-numbing errors of theological liberalism and the superficial inanities of a reactionary fundamentalism.[9] It is very important that evangelical Chris-

tians realize they do not have to choose between genuine learning and a love for Christ. The greatest command-
ment includes the requirement that we love the Lord our
God with all our *brains*.

With regard to the curriculum, this approach means
the necessary restoration of certain "lost" subjects in our
schools, a rejection of faddish electives, and a return to
an older method or approach in the teaching of those
subjects that remain. We are seeking a return, among other
things, to the study of Latin and Greek, ancient history,
the study of formal logic, and the study of rhetoric. We
seek a return to the *trivium*, a method of instruction that
proceeds through *grammar*, *dialectic*, and *rhetoric*, and then
on to a modern analog of the *quadrivium*. In doing this,
we are trying to establish a system of higher education
that equips leaders. Classical education is not necessary
for every individual distributively, but it is necessary for
our culture. In the daunting task of cultural restoration,
which is what we face, it is crucial that we train students
to continue the work we have begun. And *that* is classical education.[10]

Setting the standards high in this fashion will prevent
many modern young people from attending such colleges.
That is the point. Lowering standards is a form of contempt,
both for knowledge and for students. Students will come
to despise what they receive from their teachers if their
teachers despise what they are called to provide to the
students. No glee should be taken in excluding students,
but setting the standards high is absolutely essential to
a recovery of genuine education—

> In proof, we point to the well known fact that in those
> colleges and universities where a high grade of schol-
> arship is faithfully applied, this strictness and conse-
> quent difficulty of attaining the honors is a prime
> element of their popularity with all spirited young men,
> such as are worth having in the seminary.[11]

As we return to the old paths, we will discover why our fathers spent so much time there. We will recover an ability to answer the question, "What is a classical education good for exactly?" The spirit of pragmatic modernity, which likes to flaunt a sophisticated and cosmopolitan air, is really carrying on like a provincialist chronological hayseed. We are entirely taken with ourselves, and outside the village we all grew up in, everything is unknown; we are entirely lost—chronological rubes trying to pretend that the end of our village is the end of the world. T. S. Eliot describes the problem in this way:

> And there never was a time, I believe, when those who read at all, read so many more books by living authors than books by dead authors; there never was a time so completely parochial, so shut off from the past. . . . Individualistic democracy has come to high tide: and it is more difficult today to be an individual than it ever was before.[12]

The gift of literacy has not enabled most to get off the farm but has shackled them to Book-of-the-Month-Club selections and the local newspaper. In order to escape this, we must return to older books. As C. S. Lewis commented, "Above all, the friend to whom I have dedicated the book has taught me not to patronize the past and has trained me to see the present as itself a 'period'."[13] And elsewhere he points out the need for the fresh air of musty old tomes:

> Every age has its own outlook. It is specially good at seeing certain truths and specially liable to make certain mistakes. We all, therefore, need the books that will correct the characteristic mistakes of our own period. And that means the old books.[14]

But classical learning has Christian opponents as well. For one example, in a newsletter to his subscribers, Dr.

Gary North expressed more than a few reservations about
the current move of many Christian parents and educators back to a classical and Christian education. Many of
the criticisms are not new to those involved in this process, but this is the first public criticism of this classical
Christian resurgence by anyone of North's influence. The
writing was pure North—well-written, entertaining, in-
cisive, and seventy-five percent correct. Many of his comments were dead center: "The good old days produced
the bad new days, step by step"; "Classical education undermines Christian orthodoxy"; "The history of Christian philosophy has been one long compromise with the
philosophy of autonomous man. From Plato to Newton,
from Newton to Kant, from Kant to some cast-off liberal fad, Christian philosophers have sought to baptize
humanism."[15]

Many of North's jabs are on target—in the history
of the church many *have* fallen into the traps North iden-
tifies. But the difficulty is not with North's generalizations but with his applications. Take one example—the
charge that classical education undermines Christian orthodoxy. It certainly has, as have many other good things—
money, status, books, financial newsletters, and seminaries.
Certainly, there are cases where a classical education has
undermined Christian orthodoxy. So has *education*. But
of course, as with classical learning, such things only
undermine orthodoxy when they are disobediently
handled. Disobedience to God's law blurs the antithesis
between white and off-white. We must not resist anything
because of what *we* see following it—the *post hoc ergo
propter hoc* fallacy. At the same time, the Bible tells us the
world is filled with consequences for evil actions and bad
ideas. What is our protection? The biblical answer is biblical law—and biblical law does not forbid us knowing what
and how pagans think. It does forbid us thinking that way
ourselves.

North presents us with a false dilemma when he argues that to "force a child to learn Latin is to encourage him to accept the premises either of medieval Catholicism or the Renaissance."[16] But this all depends, of course, on what is *said* in Latin. The current literature advocating these classical and Christian schools has kept the classical Protestant antithesis and has repeatedly and overtly rejected the neo-paganism of the Renaissance, as well as the Thomistic syncretism of the Roman church. While both these other movements may legitimately appeal to the word *classical*, a third group does so as well. Historic Protestant orthodoxy is classically Protestant and the natural home of antithetical thinking. The Protestant faith is the widest and deepest part of the cultural river we call the West—we must reject all attempts to treat it as a fundamentalist, slackwater pond.

In his newsletter, North rightly admires the writing of Shakespeare and the translators of the King James Bible. But before men can write this way, they must be educated to do so. We should long for the day when believing Christians no longer write letters to the editor with fisted crayons, when we no longer debate with wooly minds and brick tongues. We should ache for believers who are capable of presenting the truths of the faith in magnificent language, rightly admired by North. But longing by itself is inadequate—we must teach and instruct in accordance with these desires. This means classical and Christian primary and secondary schools, and it most certainly means classical Christian colleges.

Once this is understood, a number of North's specific criticisms come into perspective. He says, "Classical education begins with a premise: the student must learn the classics. The classics are pagan: Greek and Roman literature and philosophy. They were based on the premise that man is the measure of all things, that man's reason is ultimate."[17] When I have taught Latin, on a number of occasions I have explained to my students some aspect of ancient mythology—which I am fond of describing as "pagan tomfoolery." Knowing what someone says is not the same thing as *believing* what someone says. So why study it? There are numerous reasons, but one should suffice. There is positive value in knowing the context of the Bible, and the context of the Bible was classical paganism. But, to heed what is valuable in North's warning, such benefits are only benefits as long as we love God and His word, and hate sin, both ancient and modern. But given that biblical love and hate, we must come to know how God gave His word to us. North does acknowledge the value of Greek study and urges Christians to that task. But he appears unaware of how Greek study, Latin study, and a study of the classical world all hang together.[18] Dabney agrees on the value of Greek, but he also shows the connection to a number of related subjects:

> But ought not the modern pastor to possess this minimum qualification? Should he not be abreast, at least, of the Ephesian mechanic? Let it be remembered that this Greek, now the classical "dead" language, was then the venacular. The educated Englishman must be no mean Greek scholar to have that practical mastery of the idiom which this mechanic had, granting that the mechanic had not the knowledge of the elegancies of Greek which the modern student may have sought out. *But more than this*: the events, the history, the geography, the usages, the modes of thought, the opinions, which constituted the human environment of the New Testament writers, the accurate understanding of which is so necessary to grasp the real scope of what they wrote, all these were the familiar, popular, contemporaneous knowledge of that intelligent mechanic in Ephesus.[19]

Dabney's point is really unanswerable. In 2 Peter 2:4, the apostle says that God threw disobedient angels into *Tartarus*—the deepest pit of *Hades*. So what is that? In Acts 16:16, Paul casts a demon out of a girl whose misfortune was to be possessed with the spirit of a python.

A spirit of a *python*? The Ephesian mechanic would know that the python was sacred to the god Apollo and was associated with the Oracle at Delphi. Well, who was *she*? And one thing leads to another. Quite simply, the background of the New Testament is incomprehensible without a knowledge of classical Greek and Latin antiquity, and understanding the New Testament as we ought to understand it will be extremely difficult without some knowledge of this background. This includes Greek, Latin, cultural practices, Roman law, etc. For just one more example:

> The unfettered quality of the governor's *imperium* is very relevant to the judicial problems of the Gospels and of the Acts of the Apostles. But first it must be established whether the equestrian governors of Judaea had the same powers as proconsuls and imperial legates.[20]

It is very easy—and very wrong—to say that Christians should study "just the Bible" or just the "Bible languages" of Greek and Hebrew. The error is analogous to saying we should not use teachers (or commentaries) to help us understand the text of Scripture. The thinking goes that we should go to the Bible ourselves "without uninspired teachers." But if we *do* go to the Bible alone, we soon discover that the Bible requires us to have uninspired teachers. In the same way, if we study the Bible and Greek and Hebrew *in isolation*, we will be very ill-equipped to understand the Scriptures. The Bible is not "The Book That Fell From the Sky." The Scriptures assume we know something of the surrounding context. If we do not, then our ignorance is not at all ameliorated because we cultivated that ignorance in the name of a high view of Scripture. Saying that we have a high view of the authority and inspiration is insufficient. Because the surrounding context of the New Testament was classical paganism, every Christian should know something of it, and every minister of the gospel should know a great deal about it.

For anyone unacquainted with our condition today, to argue for such a requirement might seem like vaporings from an overheated alarmist. But as the decades have passed, the impotent poverty displayed in our pulpits every week has only gotten worse. This is not a function of theological conservatism versus liberalism. Conservative and fundamentalist pulpits can be as inane and silly as anything found in the formerly mainstream denominations. Foolishness crosses all boundaries, and it does so because conservatives and liberals have banded together to support the common lie that a thoroughgoing confidence in the Scriptures as the very Word of God and educated sophistication are inconsistent with one another. With the false dichotomy firmly in place, liberals and conservatives line up and make their respective choices—between uneducated belief and educated unbelief.[21] But because it is a *false* dichotomy, the choices are not fixed in stone. The mindless fundamentalist soon loses his grasp of the fundamentals, and the sophisticated liberal soon embraces every loopy fad that comes out of the left-field bleachers. Classical Protestantism rejects both errors and calls us back to the standard of the Puritans—classical scholarship on fire—[22]

> Now, as to the high utility of classic culture to the educated man, the arguments which have convinced the majority of well-informed men for three centuries, have by no means been refuted by the multiplication of books in English. Latin and Greek are large sources of our mother tongue. No man has full mastery of it until he knows the sources. Translation from language to language is the prime means for training men to discrimination in using words, and thus, in thought.[23]

Ministers are called to communicate the gospel. To do so, they must understand the classical world in which God's revelation of the gospel was given to us. Christ was born in the reign of Caesar Augustus and was crucified under the Roman equestrian governor Pilate. And as ministers turn to preach the word to our society, they must address a culture whose language, literature, thought patterns, assumptions, etc. were shaped and molded by the interaction of Christianity and the classical world. A minister of the Word must have his toolbox filled with words, and he must be a master of them. Consequently, the judgment of classical Protestantism has been: a classical education is very important as an educational foundation for a minister of Christ—

> The business school is relied on, indeed, to make architects, engineers, and clerks; but real education, in its higher sense, still resorts to the classics as the foundation.[24]

One of the reasons we do not have ministers and preachers like those of the previous three centuries is found in the fact that we do not educate them the way we used to. William Cunningham makes this observation about the Reformers:

> Melancthon and Beza were acknowledged as ranking among the most eminent Greek scholars of the period; and brought at once that refinement of taste and elegancy of style *which an acquaintance with classical literature tends to produce*, and at the same time great philological learning, to bear upon the interpretation of Scripture and the defence [sic] of divine truth. Almost all of them were well read in the works of the principal writers of Greece and Rome. [25]

In his discussion of the Reformers, Cunningham shows that all of them were scholars of the first rank who ran circles around everyone outside the Protestant havens. He reveals the problem with a modern exhortation: it calls us to read the Puritans, to read John Owen, to meditate on Watson, etc., but it also maintains that life is too short to waste on literature, especially ancient literature written by pagans. North exhorts us to forget all this classical stuff and have ministers study Calvin's *Institutes*. Amen to the second part. But why read the Reformers and Puritans, and get nervous when people read what the Puritans read? Why do we want to read about what classically educated scholars did to *their* world? Sons of Abraham do the works of Abraham, and sons of the Reformers will do the works of the Reformers. This means more than just writing hagiographic biographies of the Reformers. We should *do* what they did and quit simply *admiring* what they did. And that requires classical education.

Historically, colleges and universities in America have been born of dissatisfaction. The screaming need in higher education today is readily felt by any close observer of it.[26] The current level of dissatisfaction is high. The result must be the birth of numerous colleges.

> It is common knowledge among those who study the development of American higher education that religious controversy has been largely responsible for the birth of many of the more prestigious private colleges and universities in the United States. Yale, for instance, was established by disenchanted Puritans who questioned the religious purity of Harvard. Later the Great Awakening (1740–43) stirred some New England Congregationalists to organize Dartmouth when they despaired of being able to influence Harvard or Yale.[27]

In other words, Yale was born because Harvard had slipped from its mission, and Dartmouth was born because Yale and Harvard had slipped from theirs. And in "Illinois Congregationalists and Presbyterians fought over Illinois College and Knox College. When the Congregationalists lost, there was but one thing to do: they founded Wheaton College."[28] And now Wheaton is at the heart of a compromised evangelical establishment. We have come to the time when this older process will have to be repeated.

In the long run, we have great reason for hope. The preceding observations of this booklet, thoughtfully considered, are enough to make any man an undying optimist. And why is this? As we observe the modern world, we should take a great deal of comfort from the following maxim: over time, *stupidity doesn't work*. We look at the great secular universities, and we know we do not want their barren secularism. Nor do we want the pale baptized reflections of secularism found at the Christian colleges.

Without thoughtful meditation, despair would be easy. In a fallen world, nothing can be kept pure forever. My mother attended a Bible college which used temporary buildings because the founder of the college did not want the liberals to get the blessing of taking over beautiful stone buildings. It would be easy to laugh at such dispensational shortsightedness, but the fear that institutions will fall away from their founding vision is not an unreasonable one. But the fact that we cannot build institutions that will remain faithful forever should not keep us from building institutions that will be faithful for centuries. That has been done before, and by God's grace, it will continue to be done.

So what is the need? We pray that God will raise up numerous Christian colleges that teach historic Protestant orthodoxy and apply it to *everything*. Consequently, such colleges will be Christian—in the fullest sense of that word. Moreover, such colleges will recognize that thus far in the history of our race, Christianity has had the most profound cultural impact in the West. Of course Western culture is not the only culture in the world, and we do not speak as xenophobes. The central folly of politically-correct multiculturalism is seen at just this point. You cannot teach a student to appreciate the culture of other peoples by insisting that he despise his own. The result of such nonsense is a pack of students too lazy to derive anything of value from their own culture, even though resources for learning are so close at hand. Consequently, they are supremely ill-equipped to gain anything of value from other cultures, where genuine knowledge is doubly hard to acquire. The result is a moronic rejection of one's native soil and a dabbling around the edges of other cultures—self-important tourism.

So this is what we mean by *classical*—an educated return to the cultural heritage of the West. As Christians, we seek to lead the way back; in fact, as Christians, we are the only ones who are equipped to do so. Of course, we will be accused of "turning back the clock." Exactly so.

Footnotes

1. The Paideia of God

1. For more on this see my *Surrendered Children* (Irvine, CA: Crux Press, forthcoming).

2. Werner Jaeger, *Paideia: The Ideals of Greek Culture* (Oxford, Eng.: Oxford University Press, 1939).

3. The Case Against Vouchers

1. Jack Phelps, *Against Education Vouchers* (Moscow, ID: Canon Press, 1994) pp. 9–15.

5. Does Classical Mean Reformed?

1. Martin Luther, *The Bondage of the Will* (No location: Revell, 1957) p. 319.

2. For more study, please see my *Easy Chairs/Hard Words* (Moscow, ID: Canon Press, 1991), and David Hagopian, *Back to Basics* (Phillipsburg, NJ: Presbyterian and Reformed, 1996).

6. The Great Logic Fraud

1. Quintilian, *Institutio Oratoria, Volume III* (Cambridge, MA: Harvard University Press, 1921) pp. 167, 169.

2. Dorothy Sayers, *The Teaching of Latin: A New Approach.* I have a copy of this essay in xerox form, but unfortunately have no idea of its point of origin. It is a fallen world.

3. C. S. Lewis, *English Literature in the Sixteenth Century* (Oxford, Eng.: Clarendon Press, 1954) p. 21.

4. Ibid., p. 21.

5. Ibid., p. 21.

6. Jacques Barzun, *The Culture We Deserve* (Hanover, NH: Wesleyan University Press, 1989) p. 18.

7. H. L. Mencken, *Minority Report* (Baltimore, MD: The Johns Hopkins University Press, 1956) pp. 169–170.

8. H. L. Mencken, *A Mencken Chrestomathy* (New York, NY: Vintage Books, 1982) pp. 301–302.

9. Classical Learning and the Christian College

1. One small example, a cloud the size of a man's fist, was the notorious report *A Nation At Risk*, National Commission on Excellence in Education (Washington, DC: U.S. Government Printing Office, 1983). Also see the footnotes for chapter one of my *Recovering the Lost Tools of Learning* (Wheaton, IL: Crossway Books, 1991).

2. If we were to judge from the way Christian colleges advertise themselves to prospective students, we might conclude that the purpose of Christian higher education is to make lifelong friends, eat pizza, go rollerblading or horseback riding, and oh yeah, learn something.

3. J. Gresham Machen, *Education, Christianity, and the State* (Jefferson, MD: The Trinity Foundation, 1987).

4. Charles Cochrane, *Christianity and Classical Culture* (Oxford, Eng.: Oxford University Press, 1957) p. 238.

5. Ibid., pp. 238–239.

6. Carl Becker, *The Heavenly City of the Eighteenth Century Philosophers* (New Haven, CT: Yale University Press, 1932) pp. 15–16.

7. Cornelius Van Til, *The New Hermeneutic* (Phillipsburg, NJ: Presbyterian & Reformed, 1974) pp. 42–44.

8. R. L. Dabney, *On Secular Education* (Moscow, ID: Canon Press, 1989) p. 15.

9. While the conservatism of Roman Catholicism is rejected, we should still tip our collective hat to Cardinal Newman, who at least knew what he was about. "When I am told then, by the Partisans of Universities without Theological teaching, that human science leads to belief in a Supreme Being, without denying the fact, nay, as a Catholic, with full conviction of it, nevertheless I am obliged to ask what the statement means in *their* mouths, what they, the speakers, understand by the word 'God.'

Let me not be thought offensive, if I question, whether it means the same thing on the two sides of the controversy. With us Catholics, *as with the first race of Protestants*, as with Mahometans, and all Theists, the word contains, as I have already said, *a theology in itself.*" John Newman, *The Idea of a University* (New York, NY: Longmans, Green, and Co., 1907) pp. 35–36. The emphases here are mine.

10. "The task of the modern educator is not to cut down jungles but to irrigate deserts. The right defence [sic] against false sentiments is to inculcate just sentiments. By starving the sensibility of our pupils we only make them easier prey to the propagandist when he comes. For famished nature will be avenged and a hard heart is no infallible protection against a soft head." C. S. Lewis, *The Abolition of Man* (New York, NY: Macmillan, 1947) p. 24.

11. R. L. Dabney, "Memorial on Theological Education" in *Discussions, Evangelical* (Harrisonburg, VA: Sprinkle Publications, 1982) p. 63.

12. T. S. Eliot, "Religion and Literature," *Essays Ancient and Modern* (New York, NY: Harcourt-Brace, 1932) p. 109.

13. C. S. Lewis, *The Allegory of Love* (Oxford, Eng.: Oxford University Press, 1936) p. viii.

14. C. S. Lewis, "On the Reading of Old Books," *God in the Dock* (Grand Rapids, MI: Eerdmans, 1970) p. 202.

15. Gary North, *Institute for Christian Economics* newsletter, May 1995.

16. Ibid.

17. Ibid.

18. On the practical side, the study of Greek is much simpler when it follows the study of Latin. The grammar of the two languages operate in much the same way. And for those Latin students who never go on to any other language study (including continued study of Latin) the benefits for mastery of English are profound. Over half the words in English come from Latin.

19. R. L. Dabney, "A Thoroughly Educated Ministry," in *Discussions, Evangelical* (Harrisonburg, VA: Sprinkle Publications, 1982) p. 664. Emphasis mine.

20. A. N. Sherwin-White, *Roman Law and Roman Society in the New Testament* (Grand Rapids, MI: Baker, 1963) p. 5. Also see William MacKenzie, "The Place of Greek and Latin in the Preparation for the Ministry," in *Latin and Greek in American Education* (New York, NY: MacMillian, 1911) p. 154.

21. A recent article in the *Christian Activist* related the joke about what an evangelical said to a liberal, "I'll call you a Christian if you call me a scholar."

22. In this respect, I consider J. Gresham Machen to be the last of the Puritans. He was the last great public figure who combined, in rigorous balance, classical intellectual rigor and burning evangelical zeal. If God is merciful to us, he will not always be "the last of the Puritans."

23. R. L. Dabney, "A Thoroughly Educated Ministry" in *Discussions, Evangelical* (Harrisonburg, VA: Sprinkle Publications, 1982) p. 660.

24. Ibid., p. 666.

25. William Cunningham, *The Reformers and the Theology of the Reformation* (Carlisle, PA: Banner of Truth, 1989) p. 603.

26. The need is obvious, and for many Christian families the situation is desperate. As desperate parents search for a Christian college, many are considering various alternative forms of college education. Among the possibilities, one of the more frequently mentioned is the idea of establishing true Christian colleges "on-line." But it is my conviction that there are severe limits to the possibilities of such an Internet College. No doubt numerous efforts will be made to build this new way of higher education, marrying the old with the new; but still, *mutatis mutandis*, it is my conviction that such efforts will fall far short of providing what the older colleges provided.

27. Wilson Thompson, *Small Colleges and Goal Dis-*

placement (unpublished doctoral thesis, 1978).

28. Frederick Rudolph, as quoted by Wilson Thompson, *Small Colleges,* p. 5.